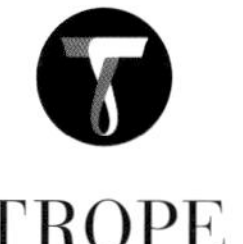

TROPE

TROPE SIGNATURES

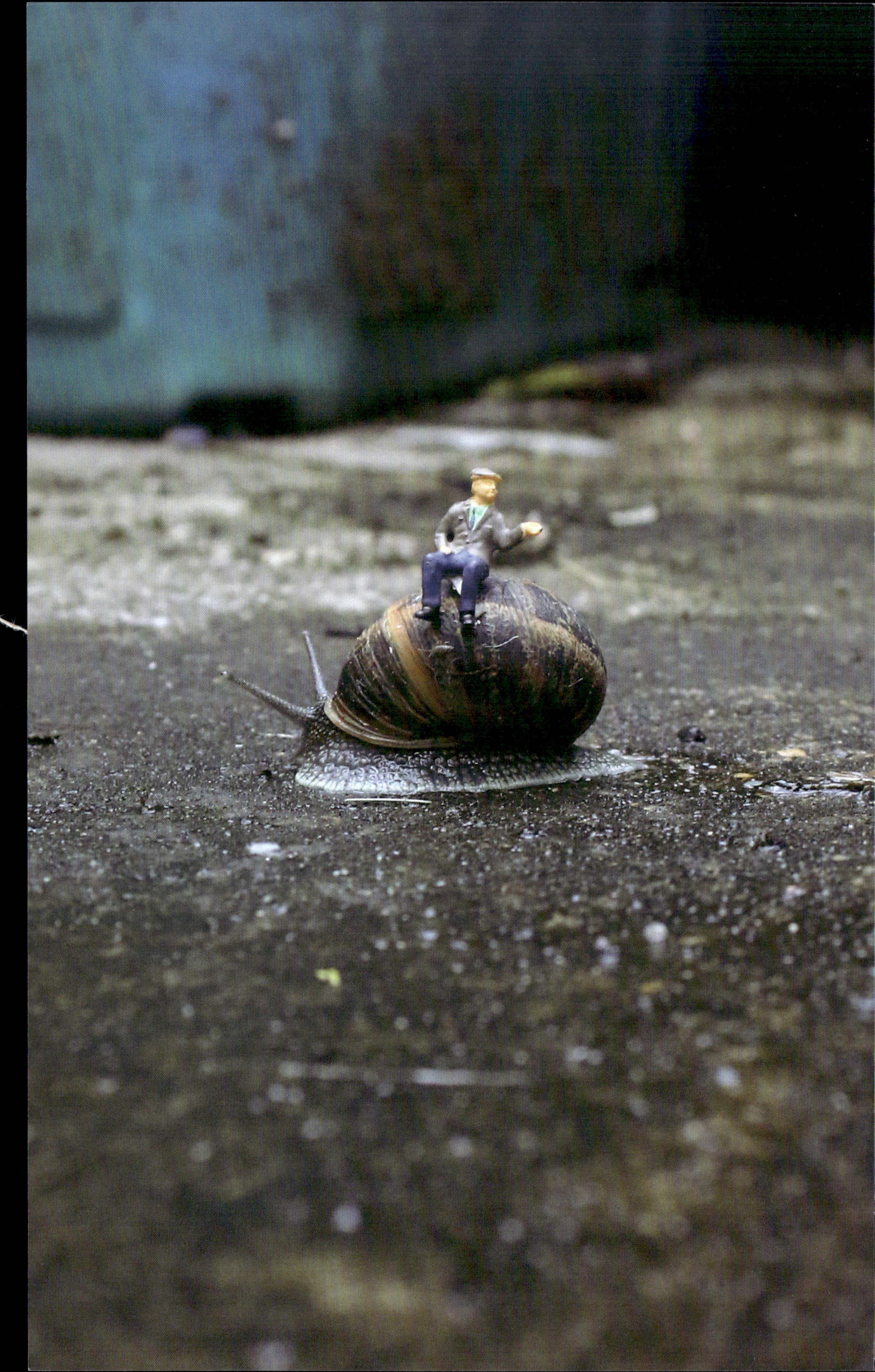

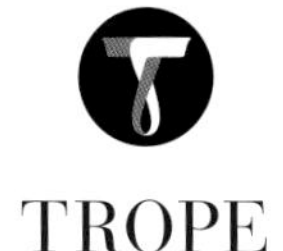

TROPE

SMALL WORLD

STEVE ROLFE

TROPE SIGNATURES

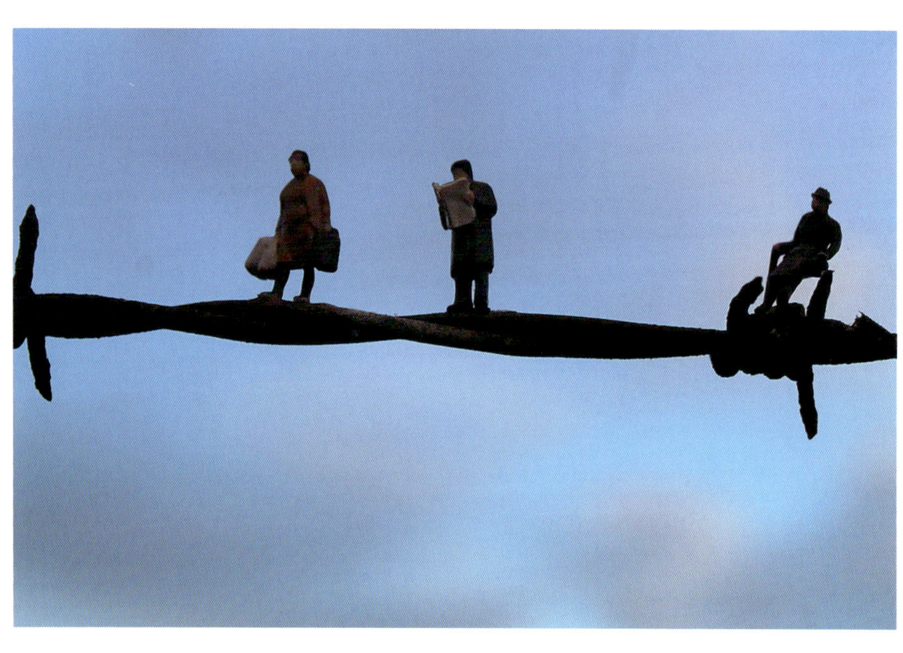

Small World introduces photographer Steve Rolfe, whose tiny scenes echo real life at an impossible scale. His whimsical images feature miniature model figures in real world situations that create an unusual juxtaposition. While they may only be several centimeters tall, they are giants in Steve's photographic story.

Steve came to photography in mid-life, after a career in the UK's civil service. A chance encounter with a book of street photography led him to pick up his wife's camera and begin shooting the world around him. What began as a hobby to help explore his creative side outside of office work eventually became a full-time career.

Steve's unique imagery is inspired by life. He has a keen eye for finding something unusual in the mundane. Sometimes witty, sometimes earnest, Steve's images invite us to take a new look at the things around us – from a puddle on the sidewalk, to the discarded fast food container, to a half-eaten candy bar. I hope *Small World* will make you believe the magic of life's little moments truly are all around us.

Sam Landers

Editor

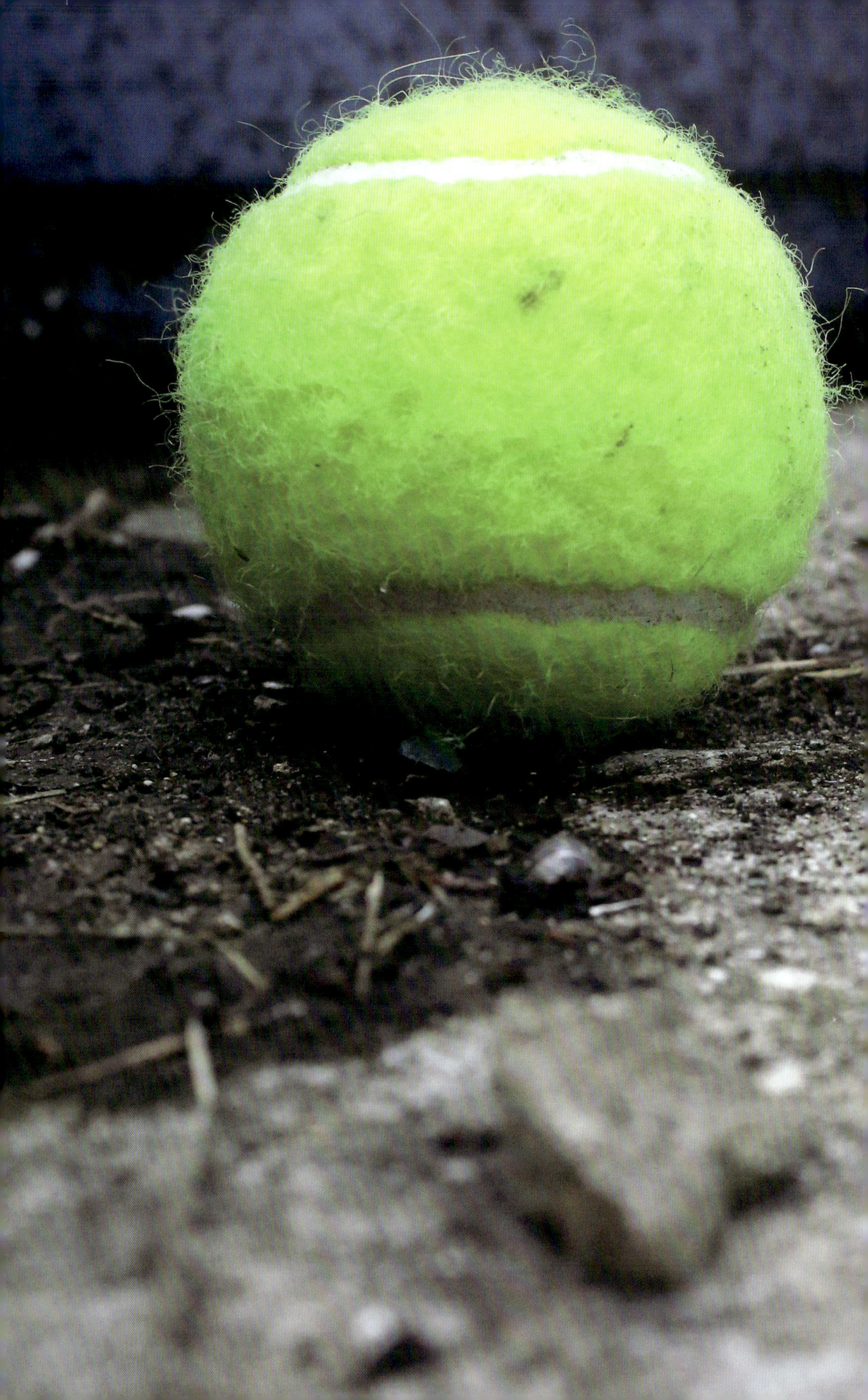

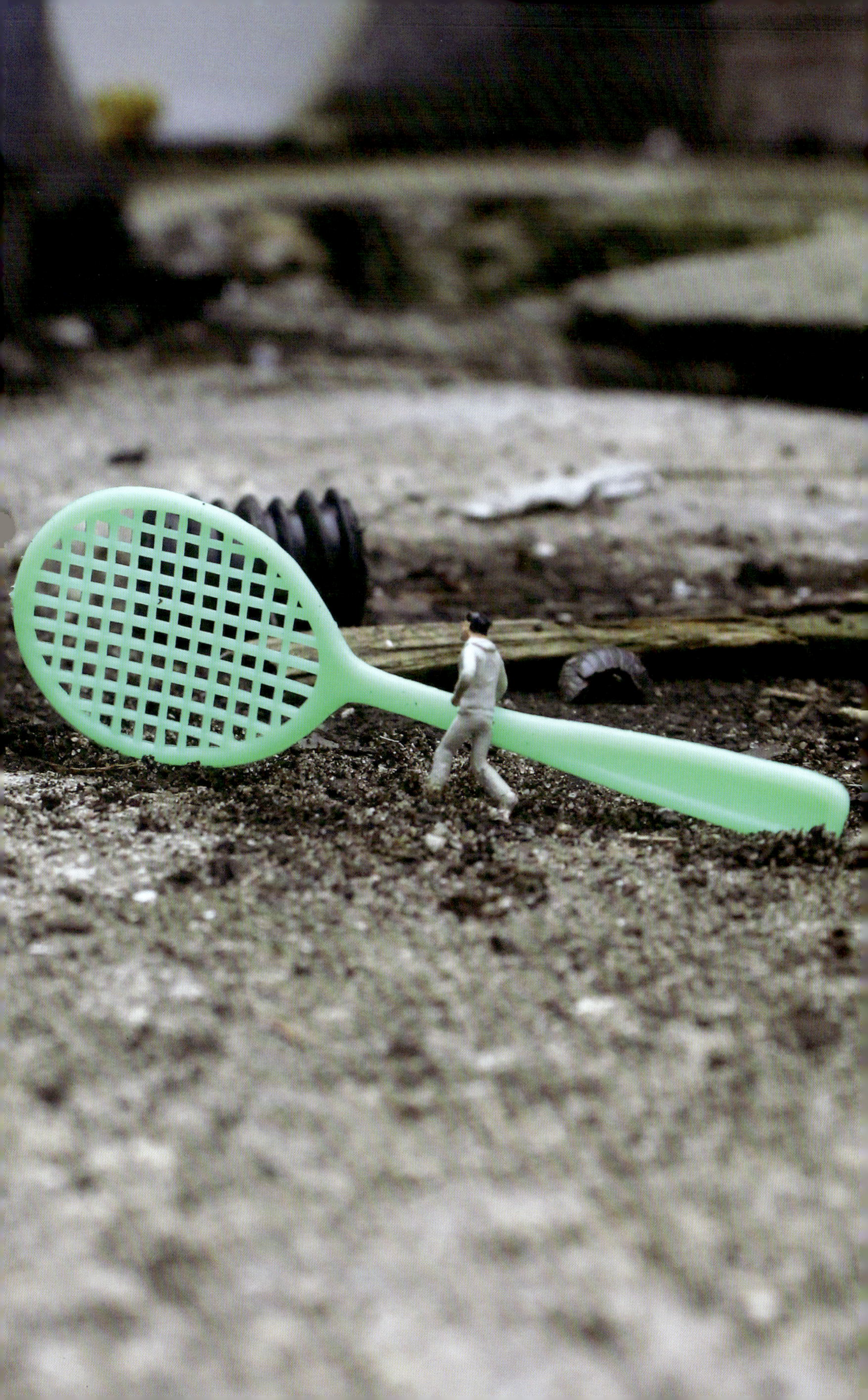

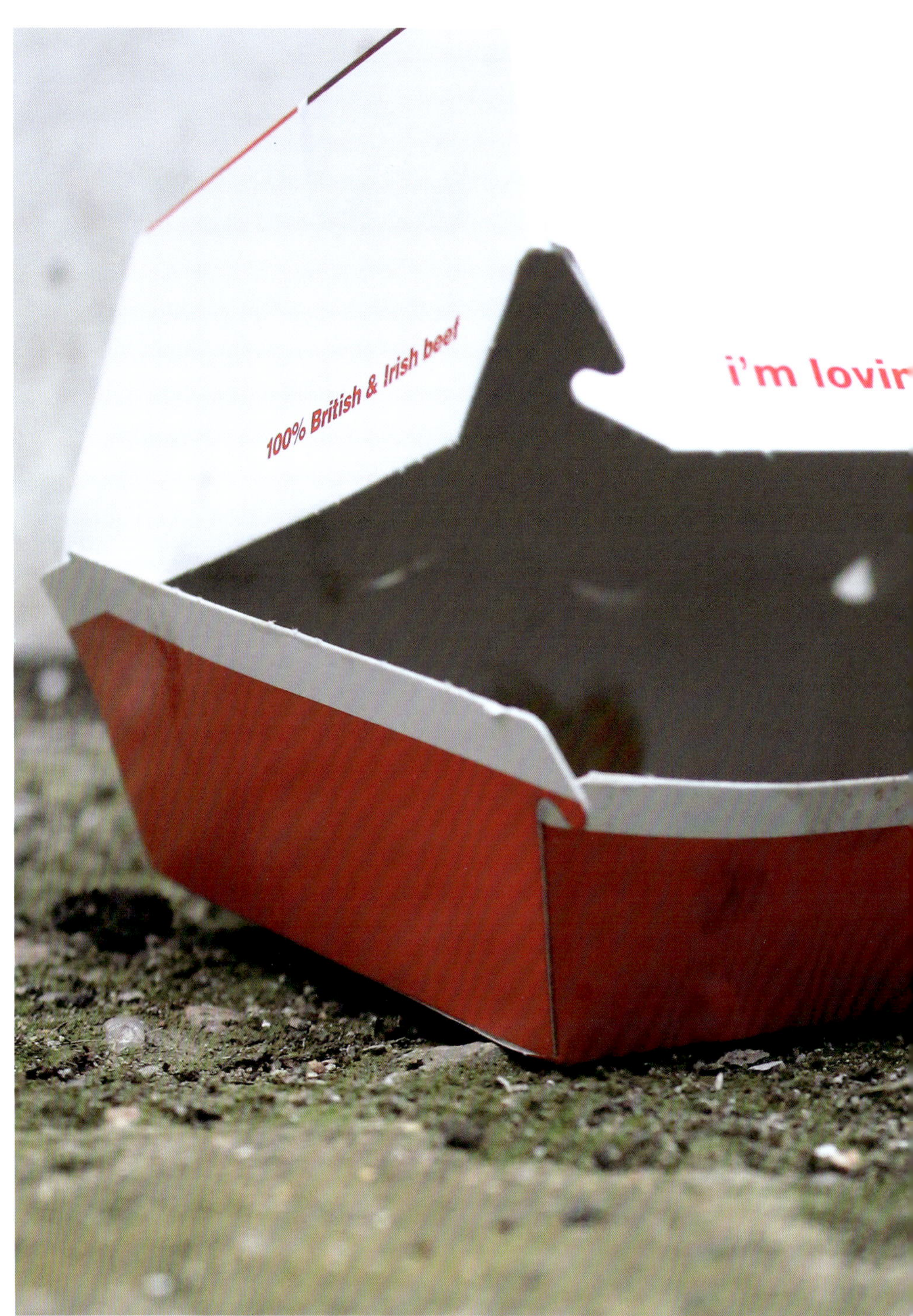

100% British & Irish beef
i'm lovin

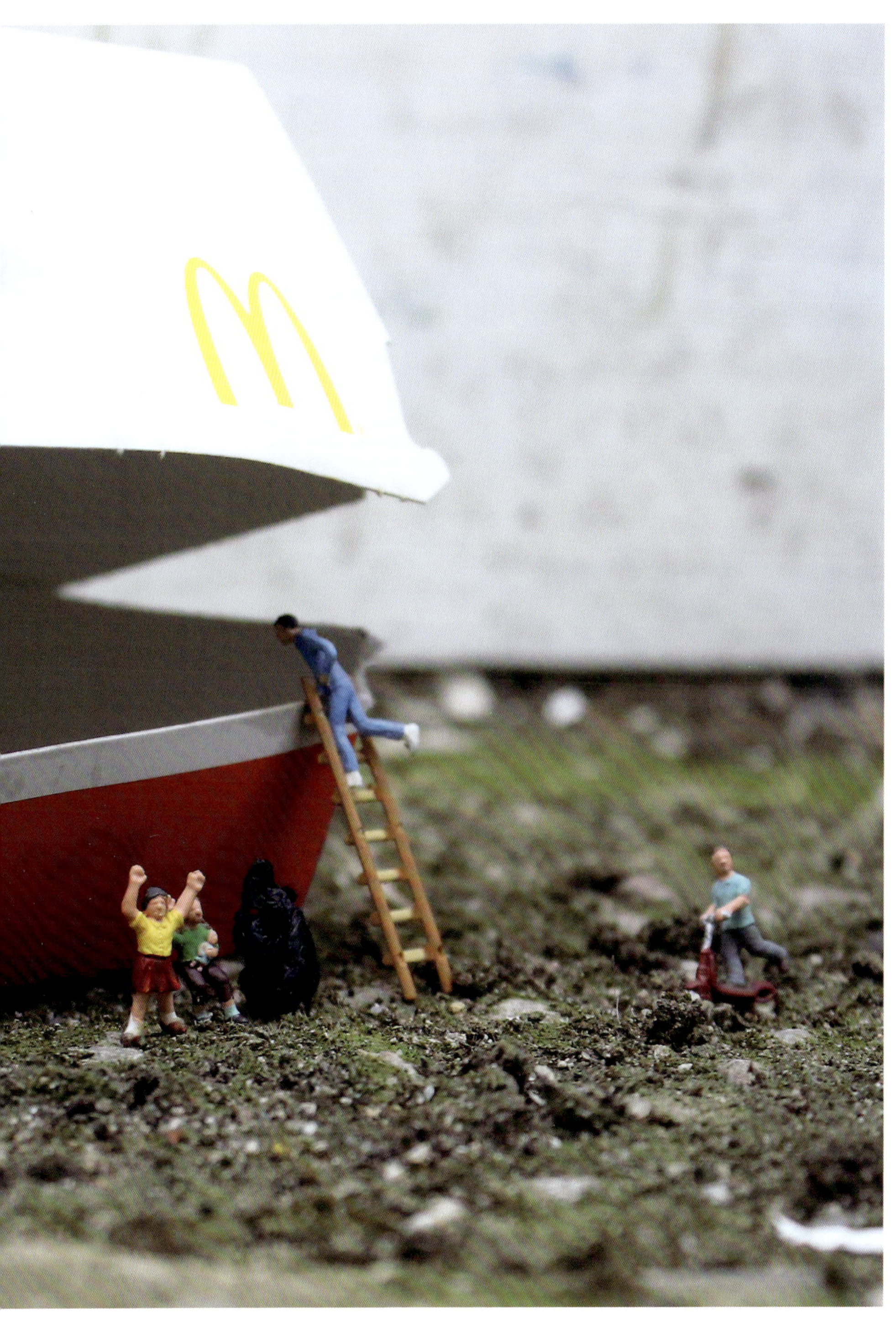

New Home

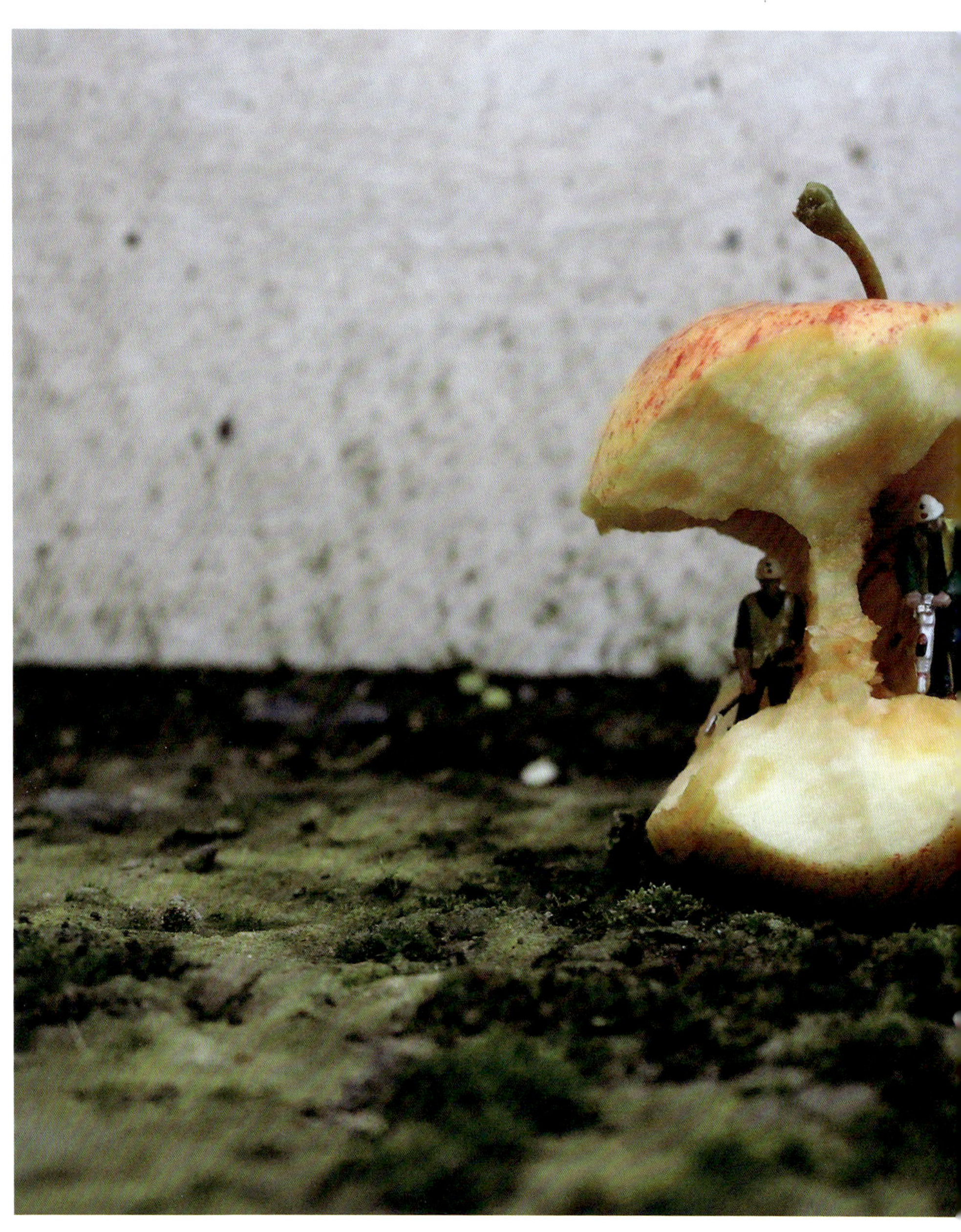

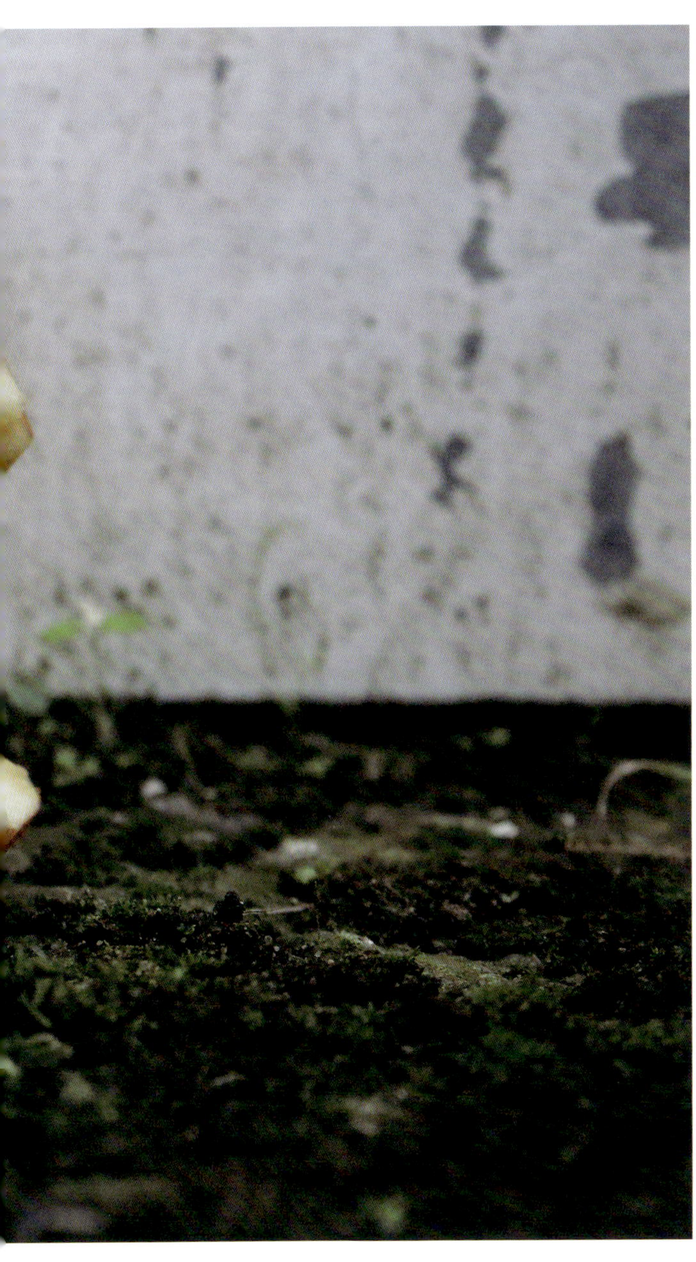

Core Workers

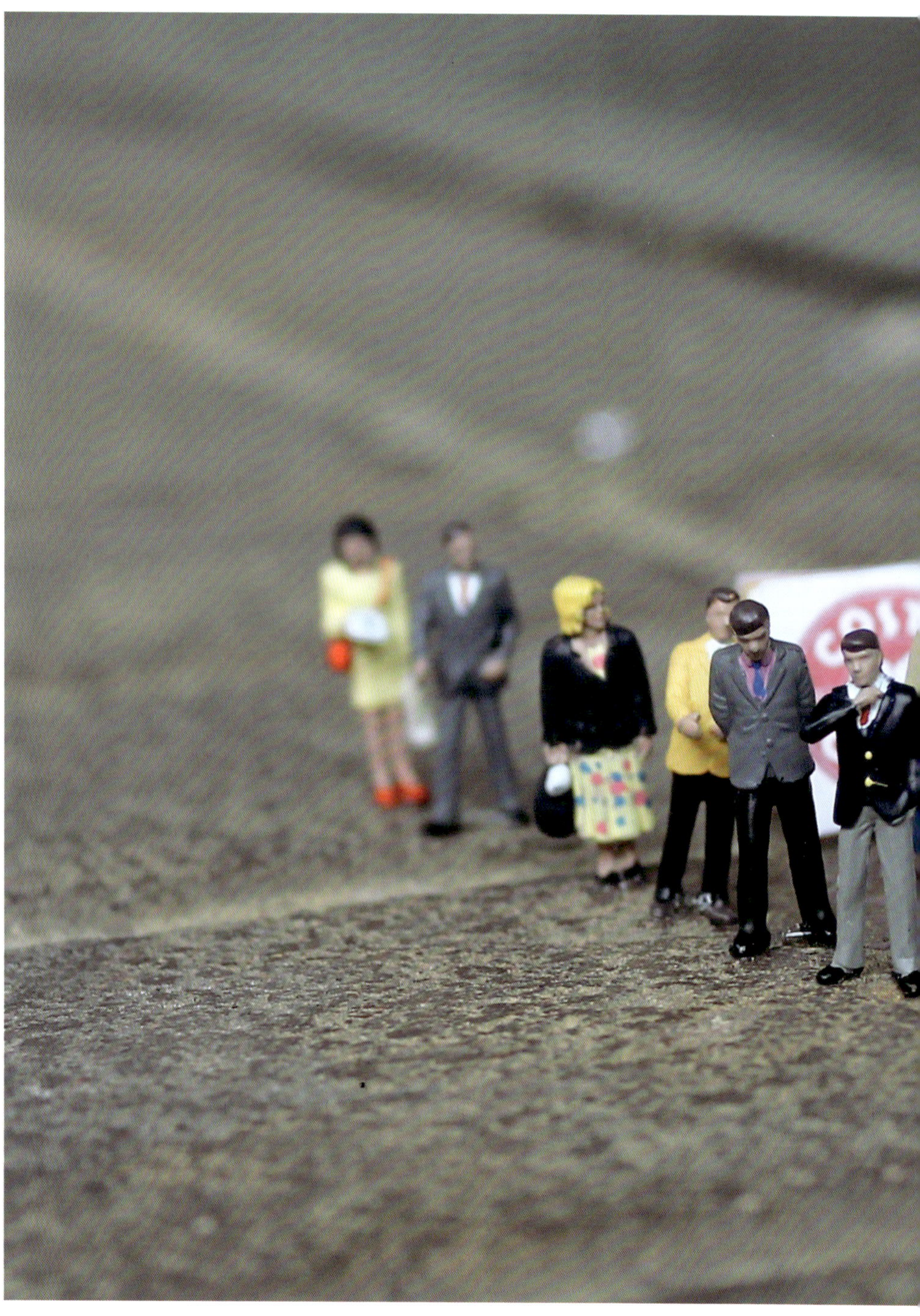

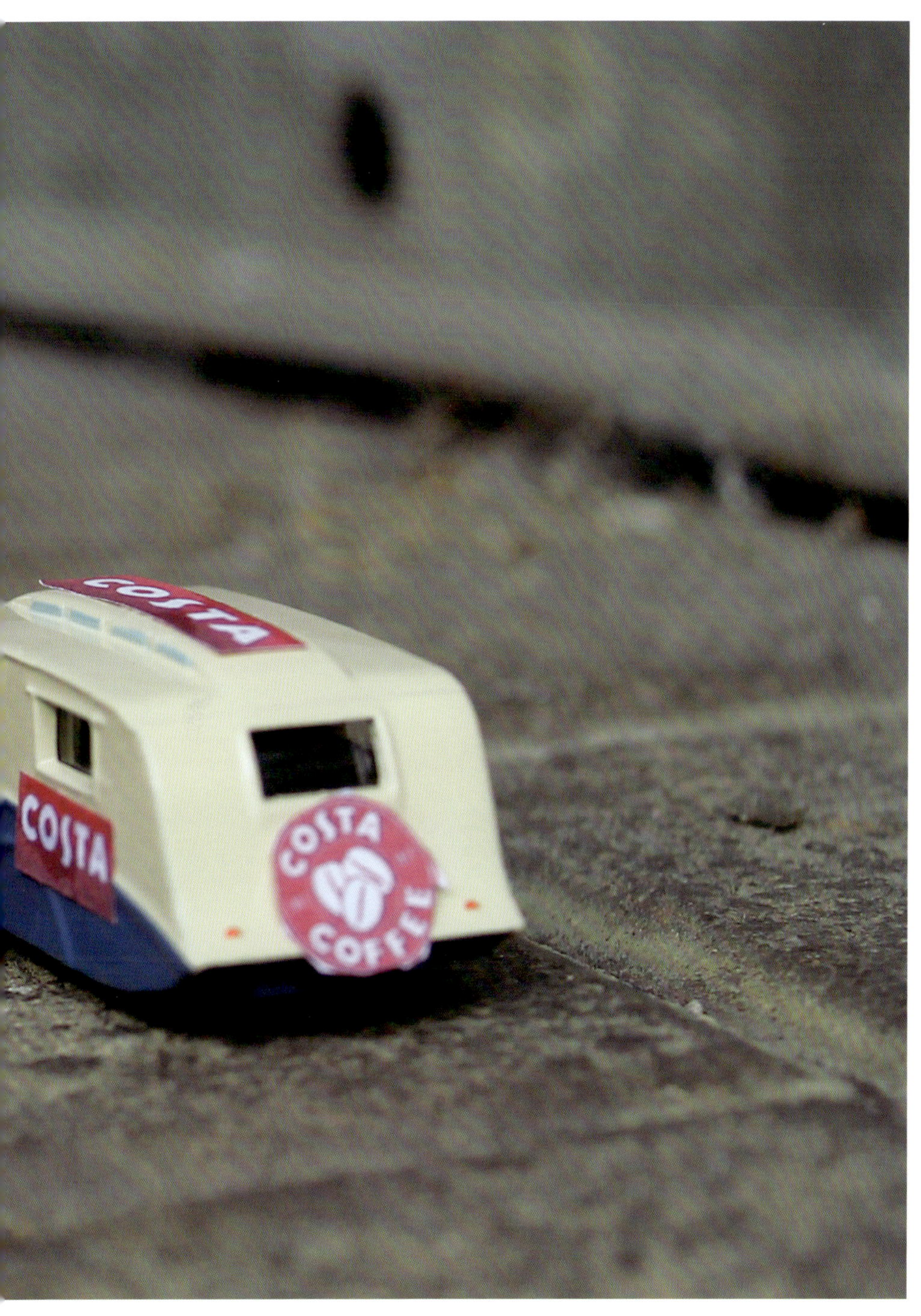

Get in Line!

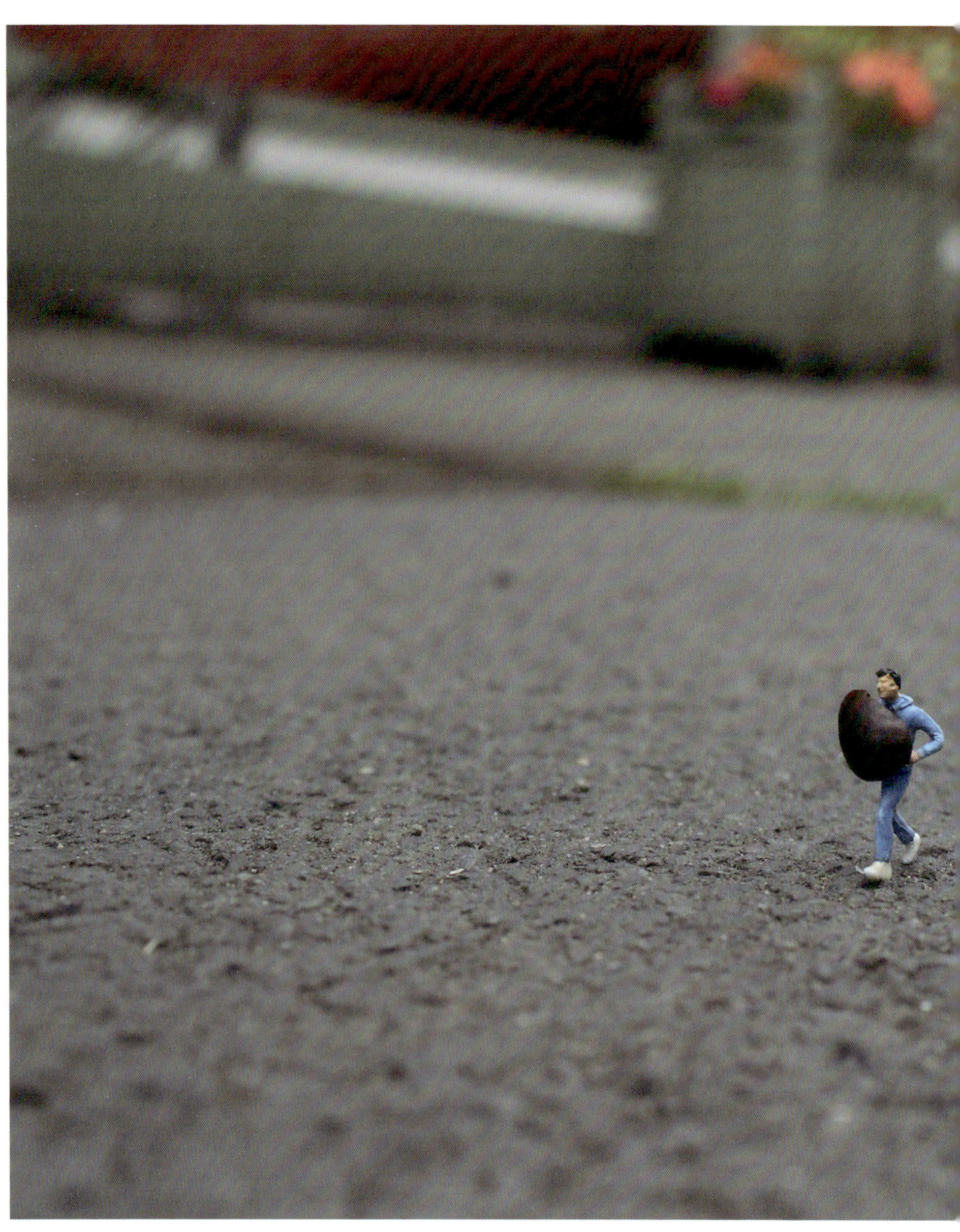

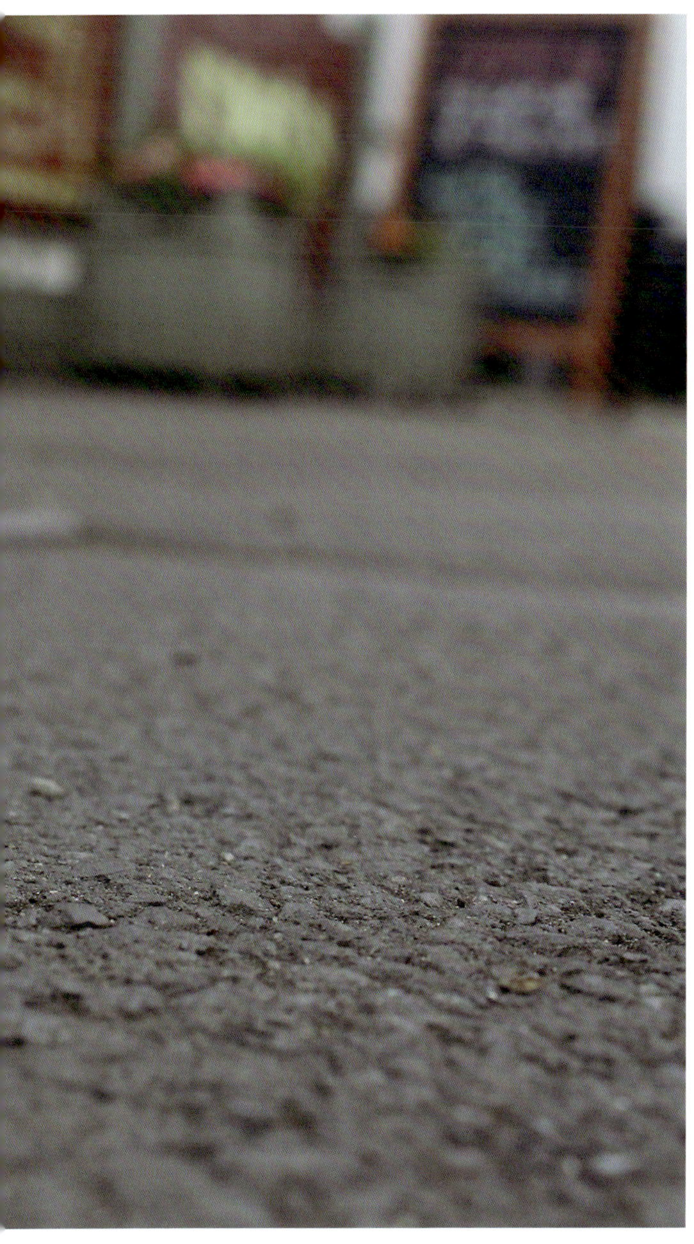

Coffee To-Go

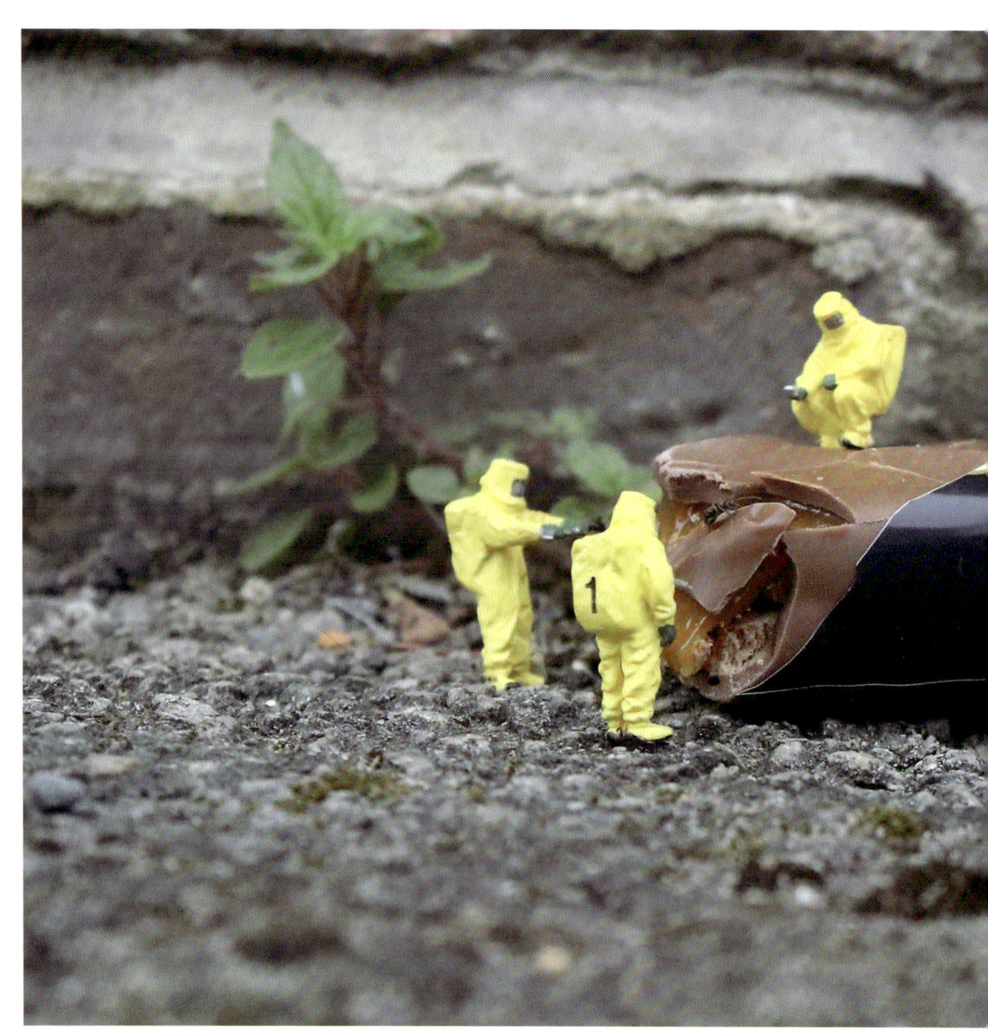

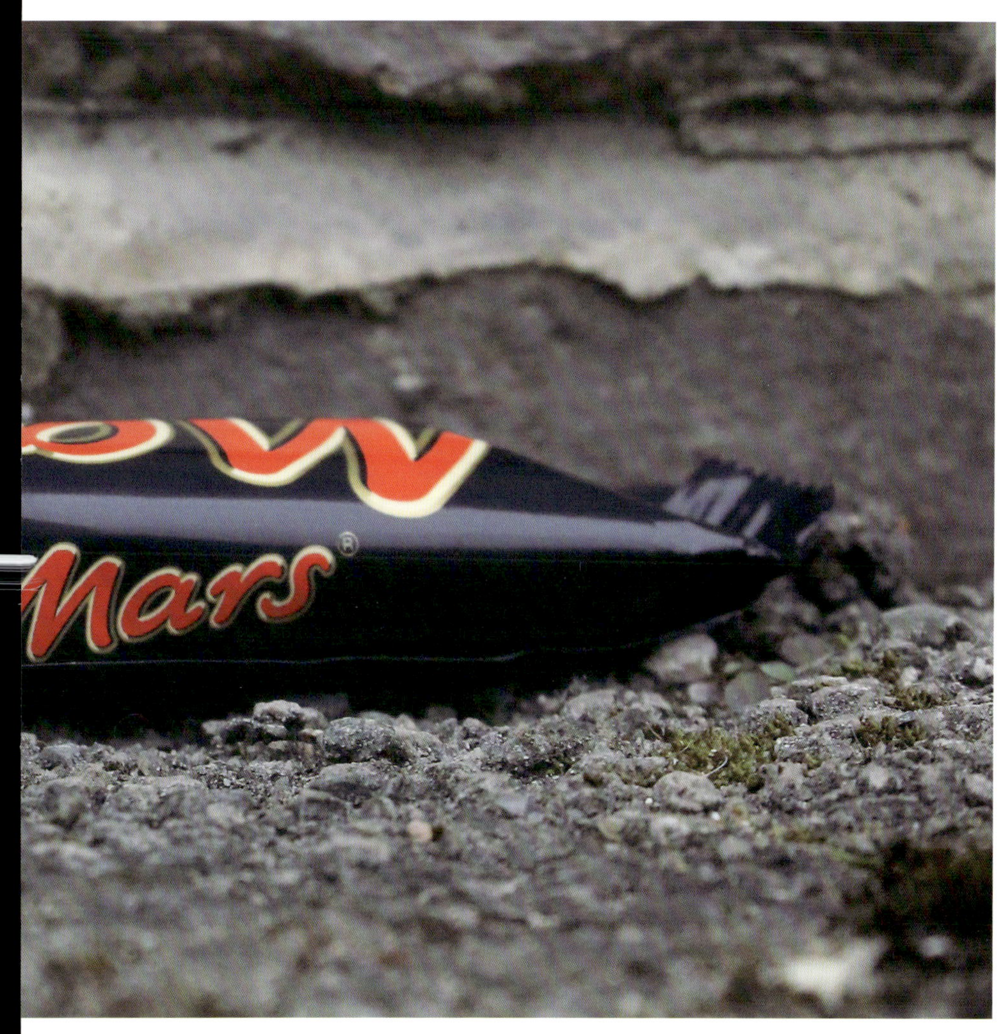

Mars Expedition

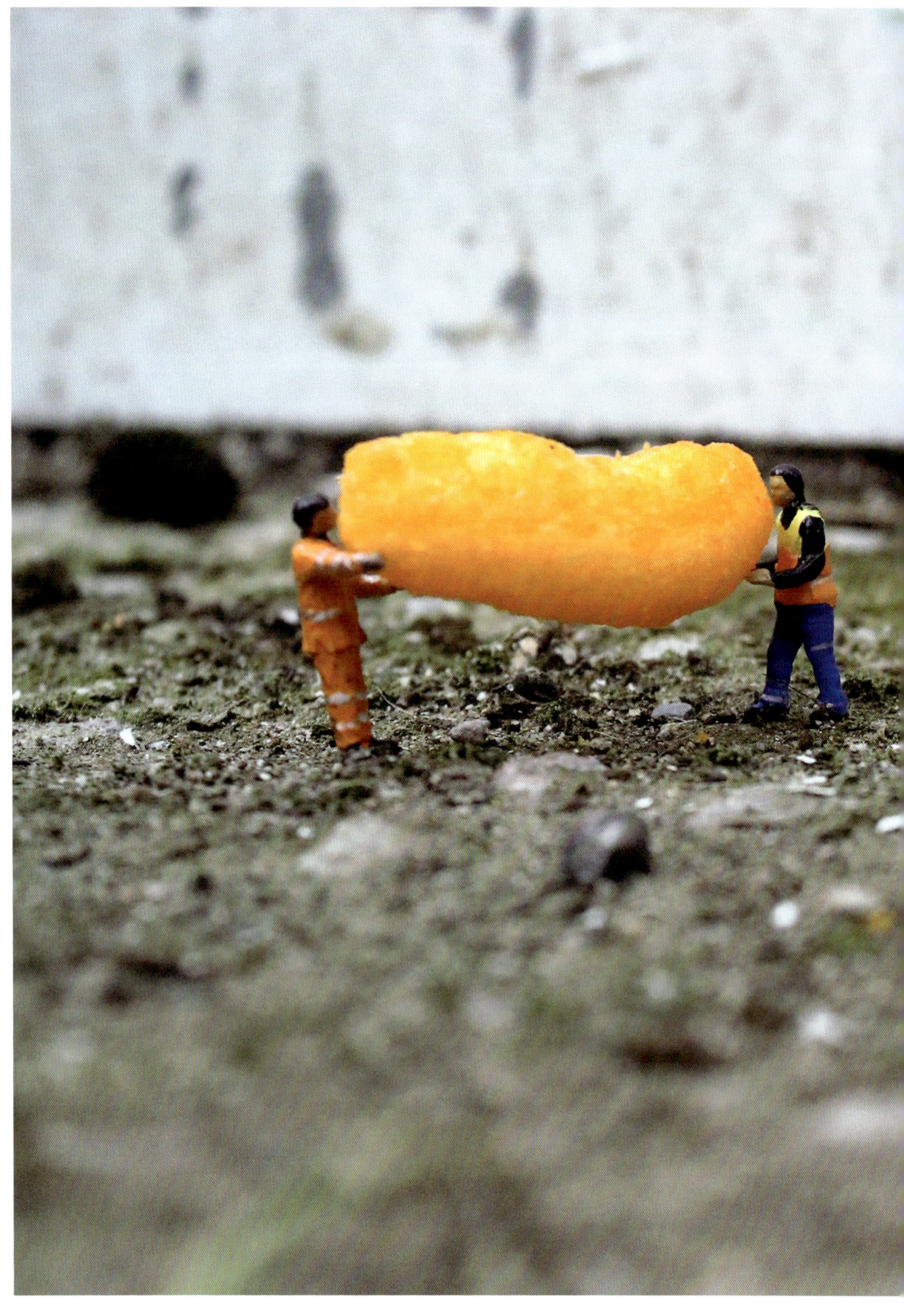

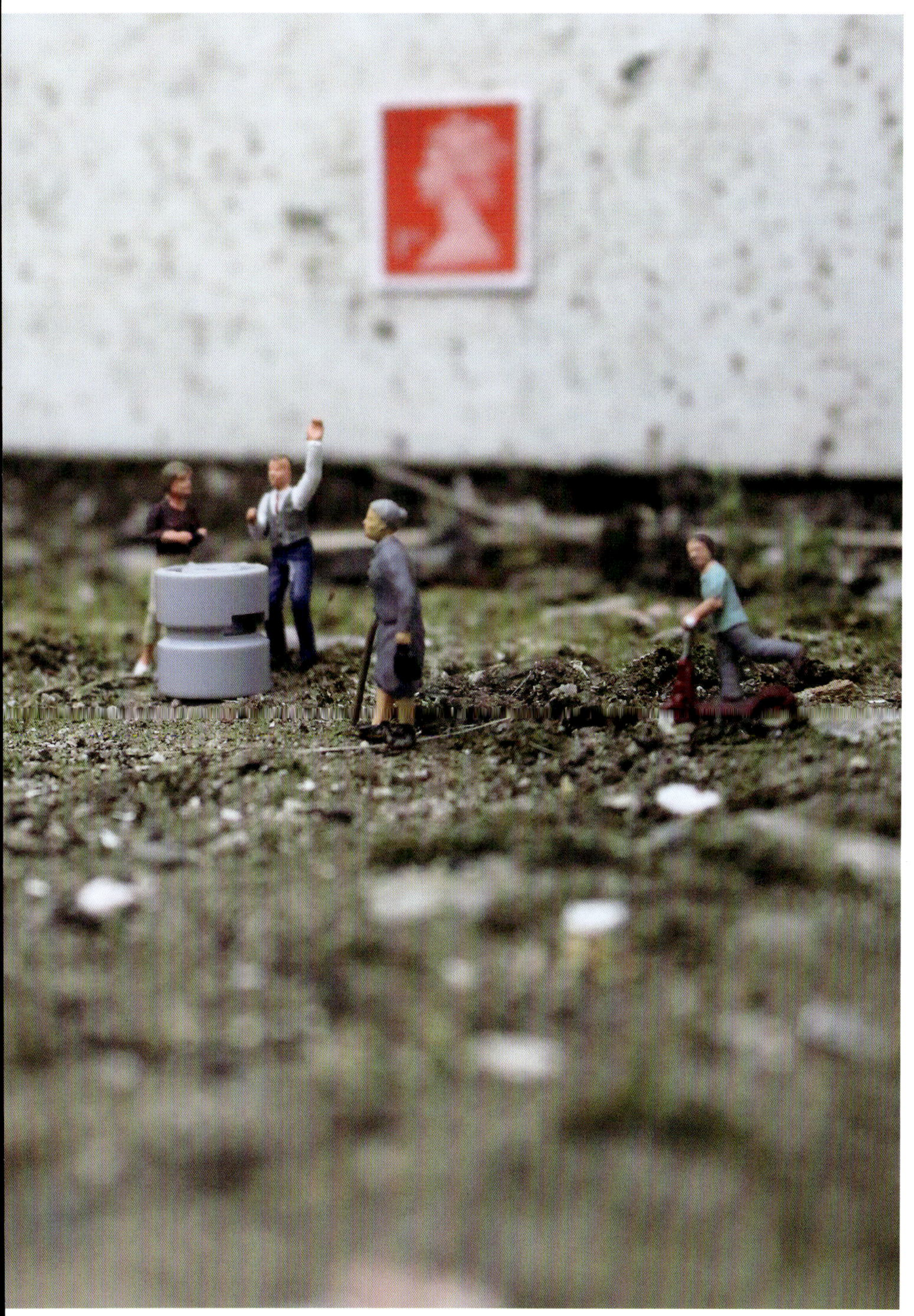

God Save the Queen!

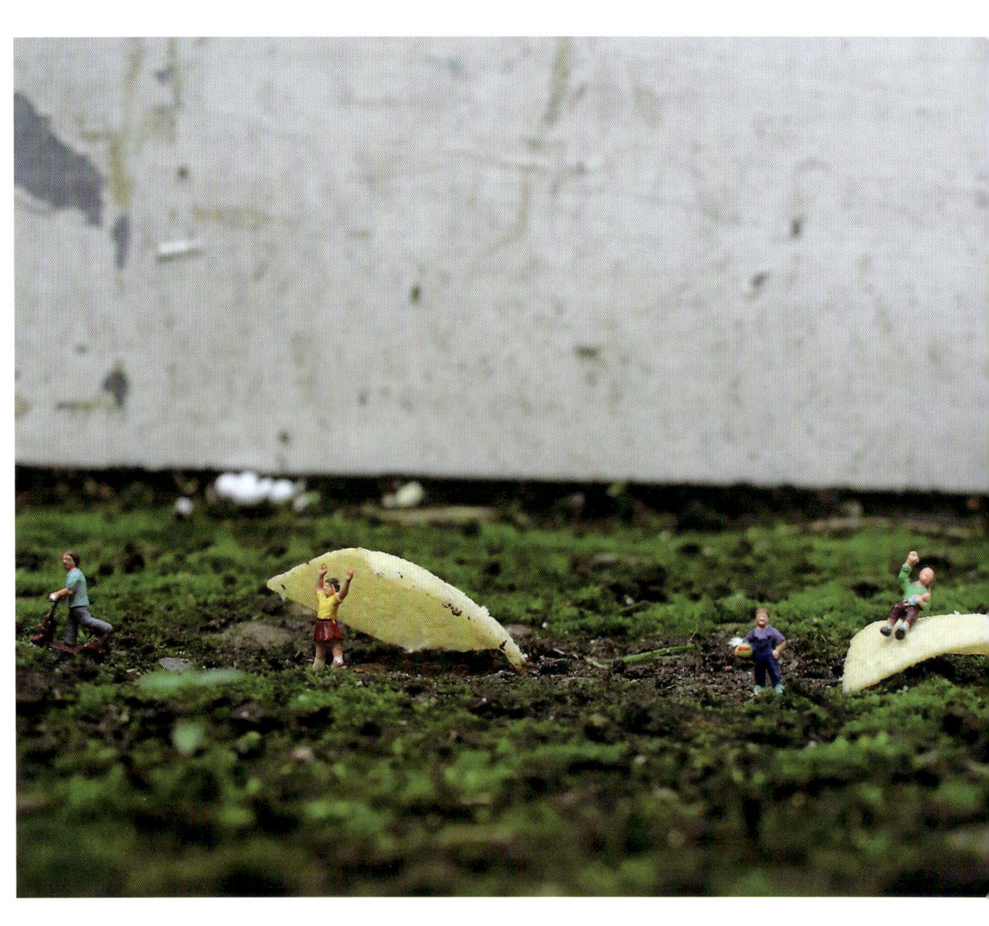

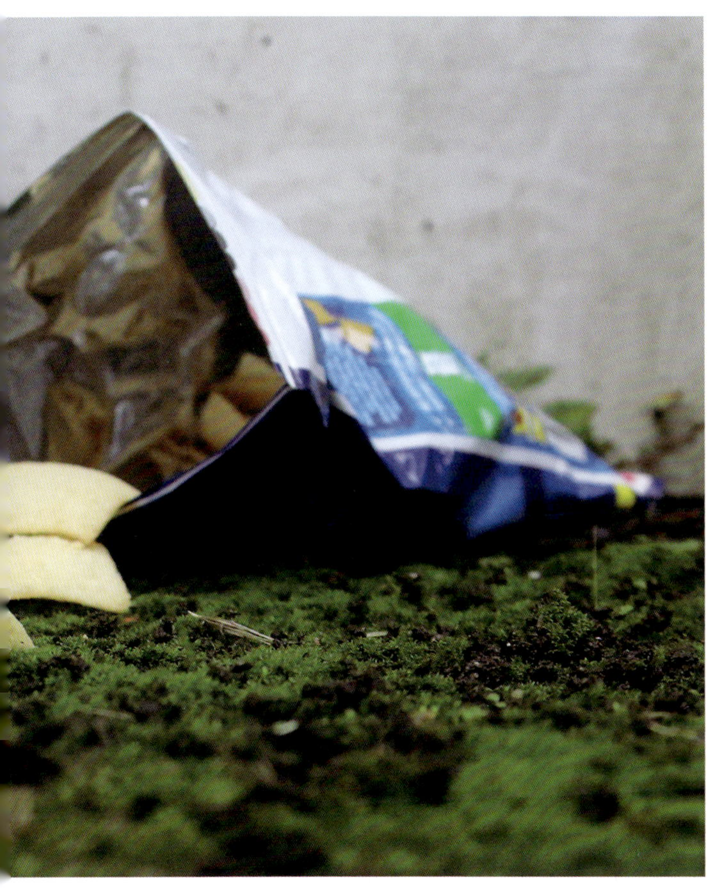

School Lunch

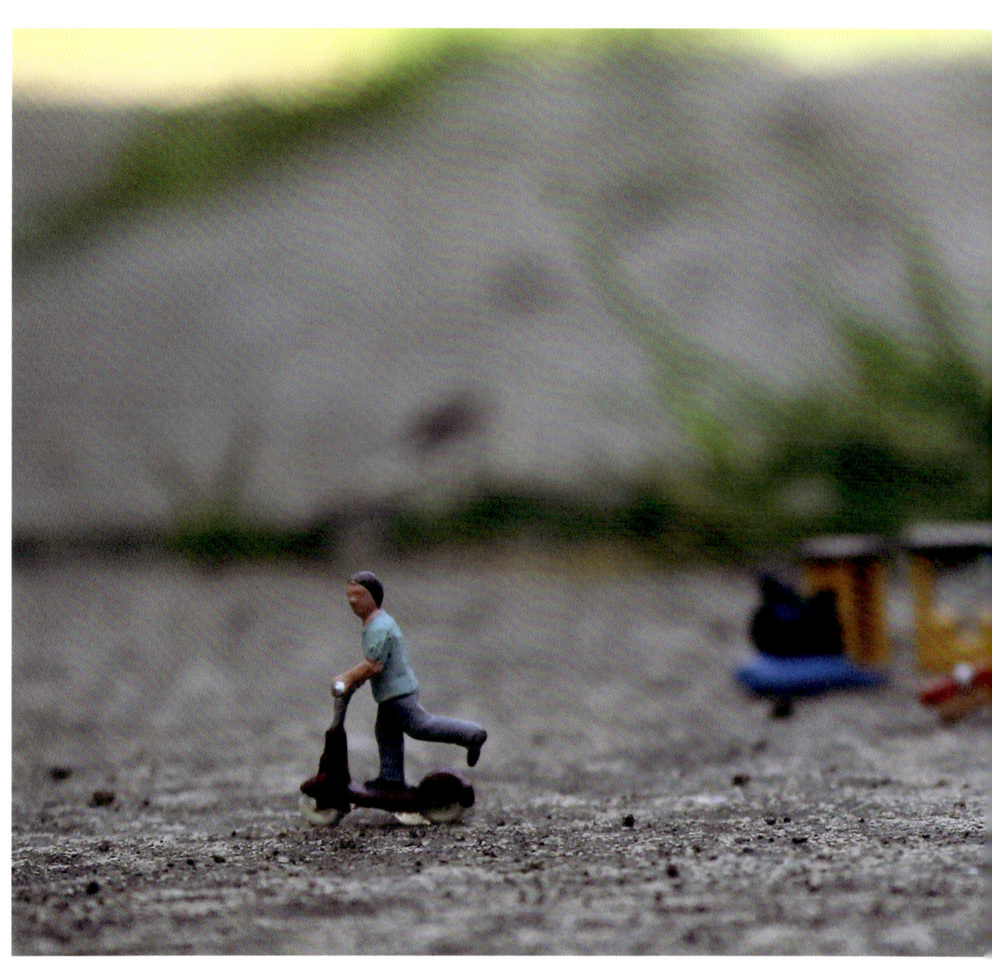

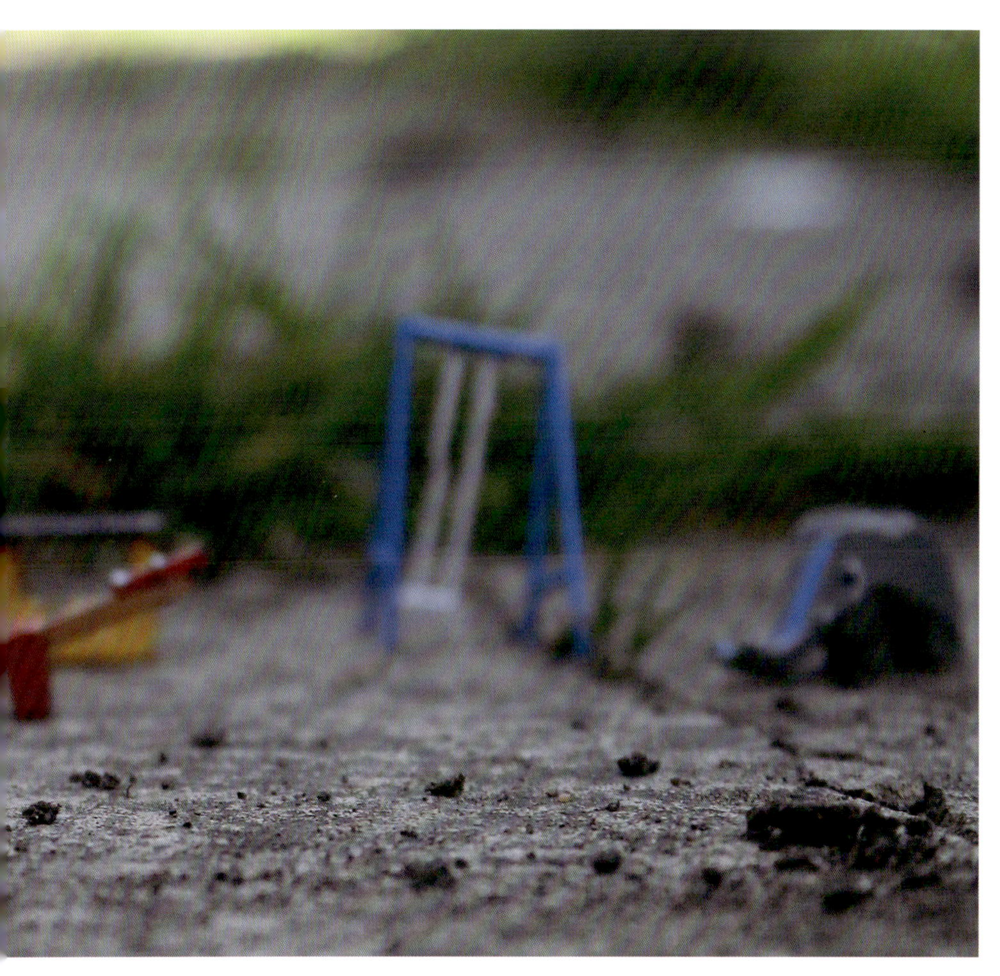

Daily Commute

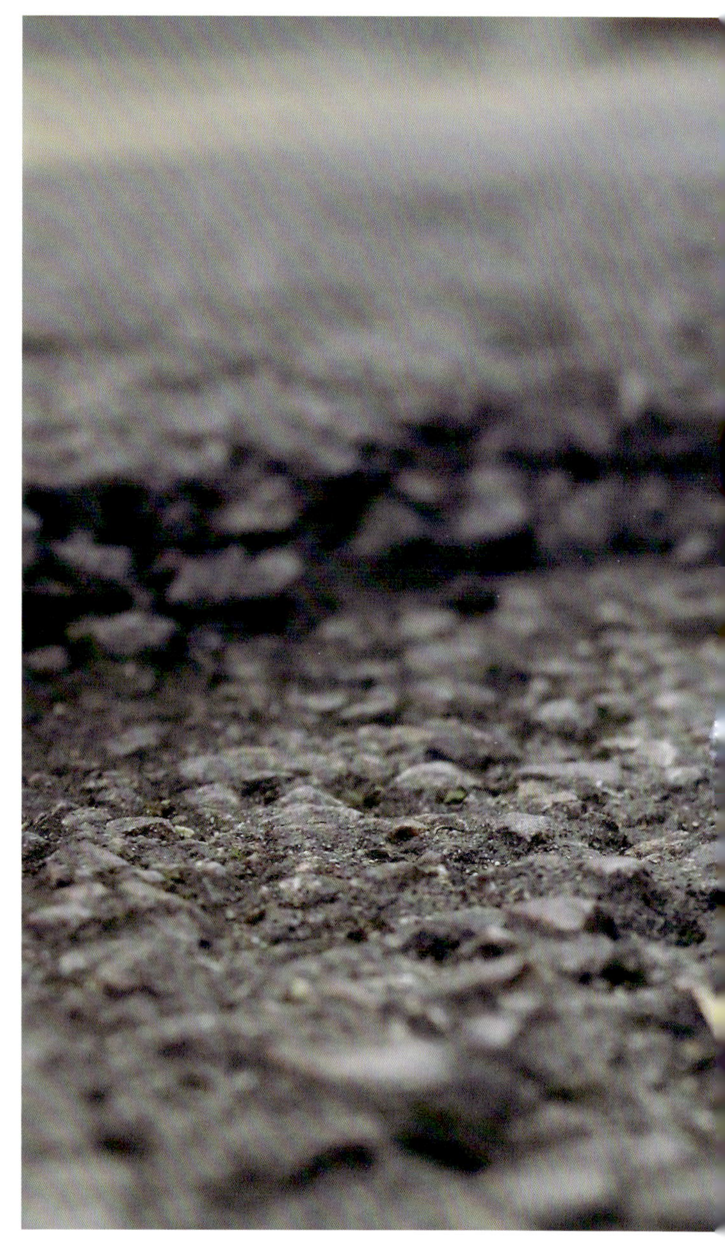

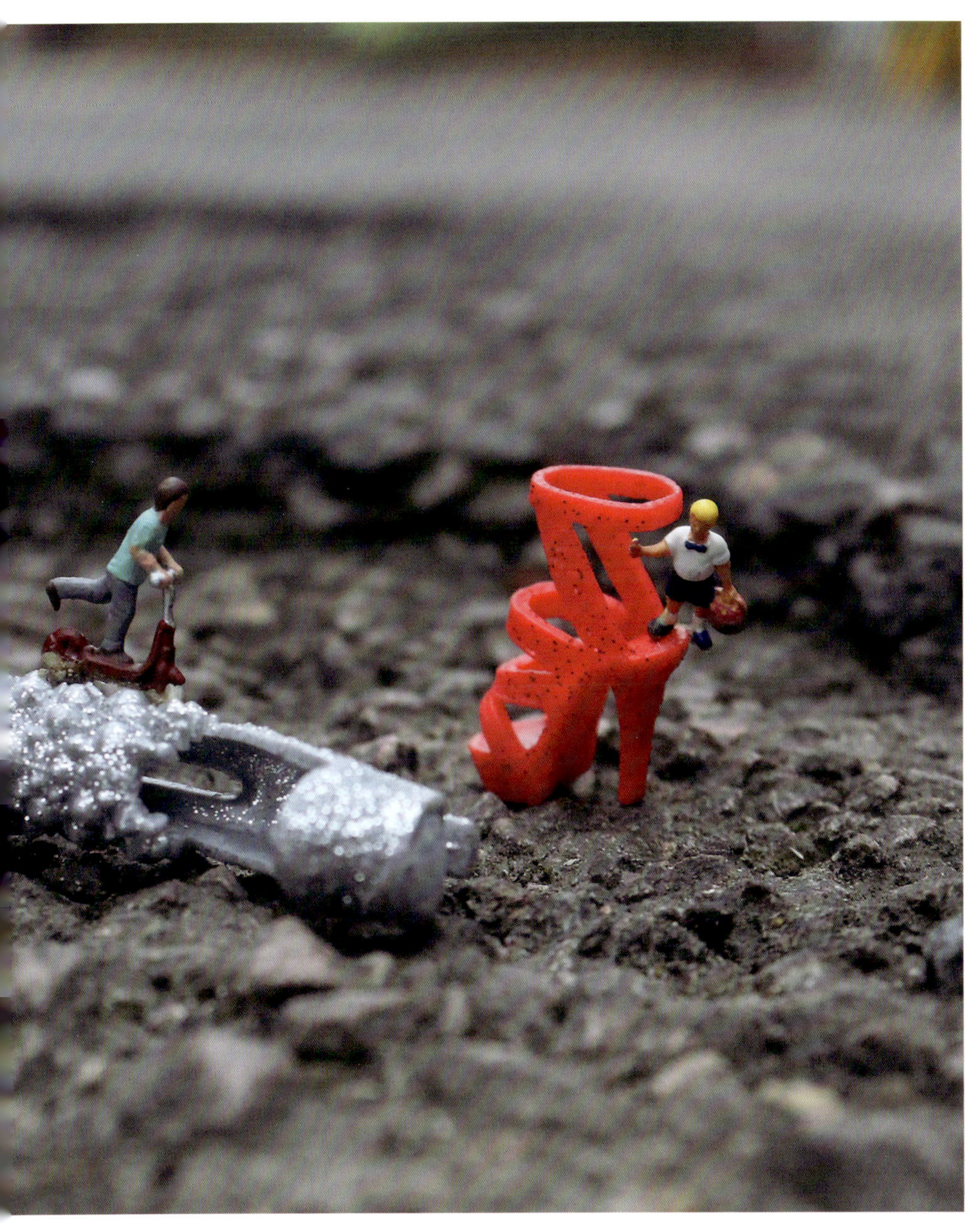

Obstacle Course

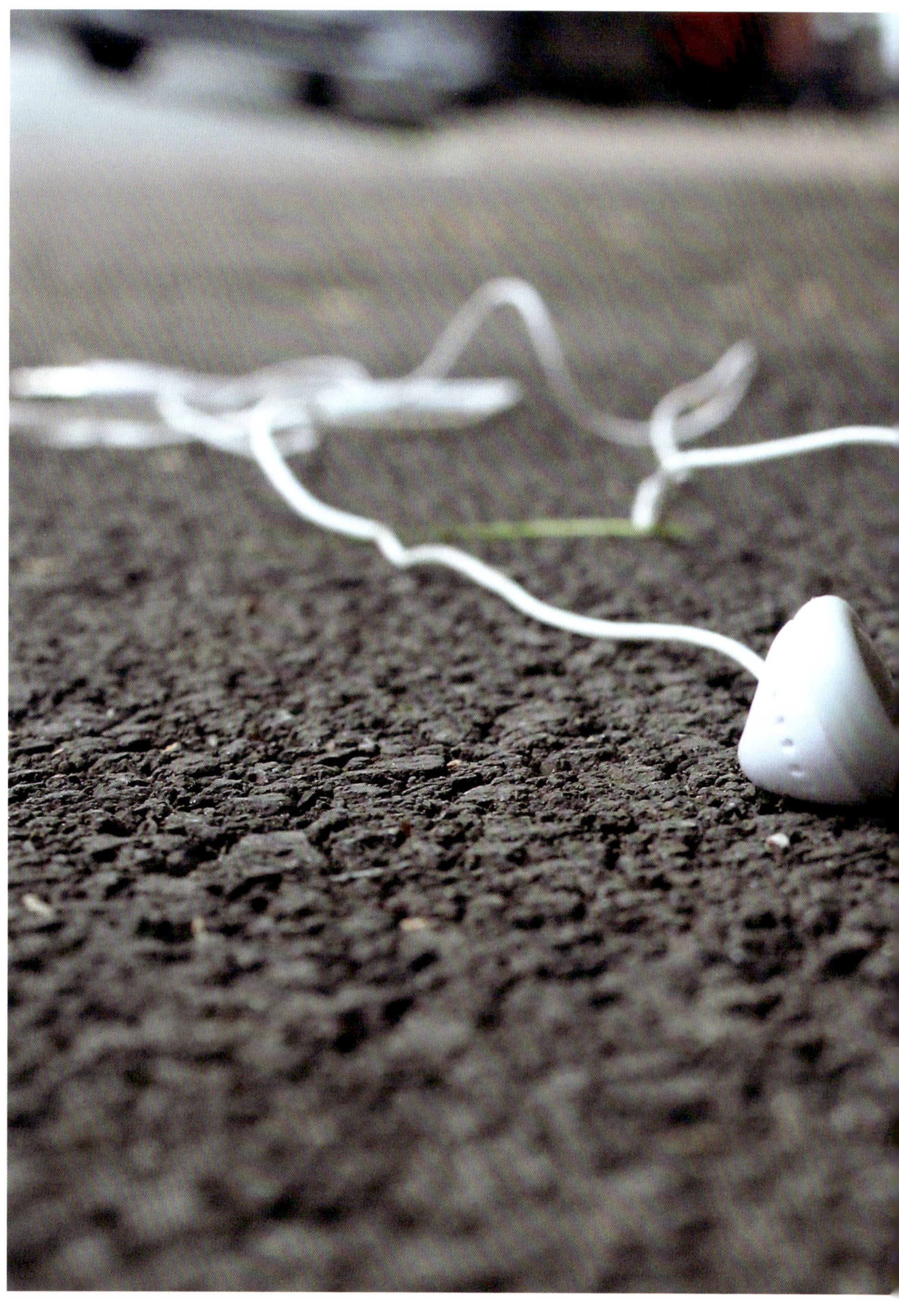

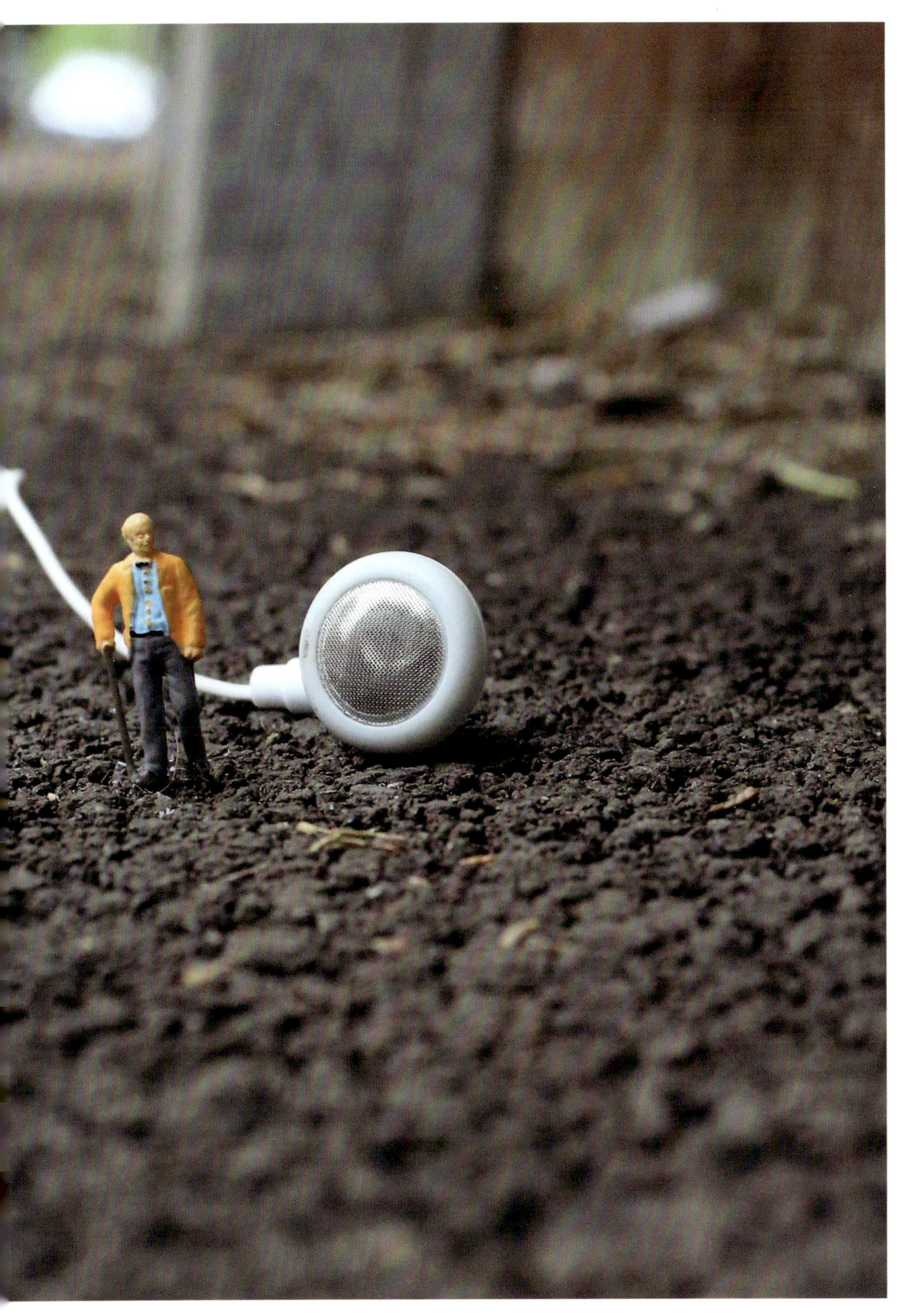

Grandpa's Boombox

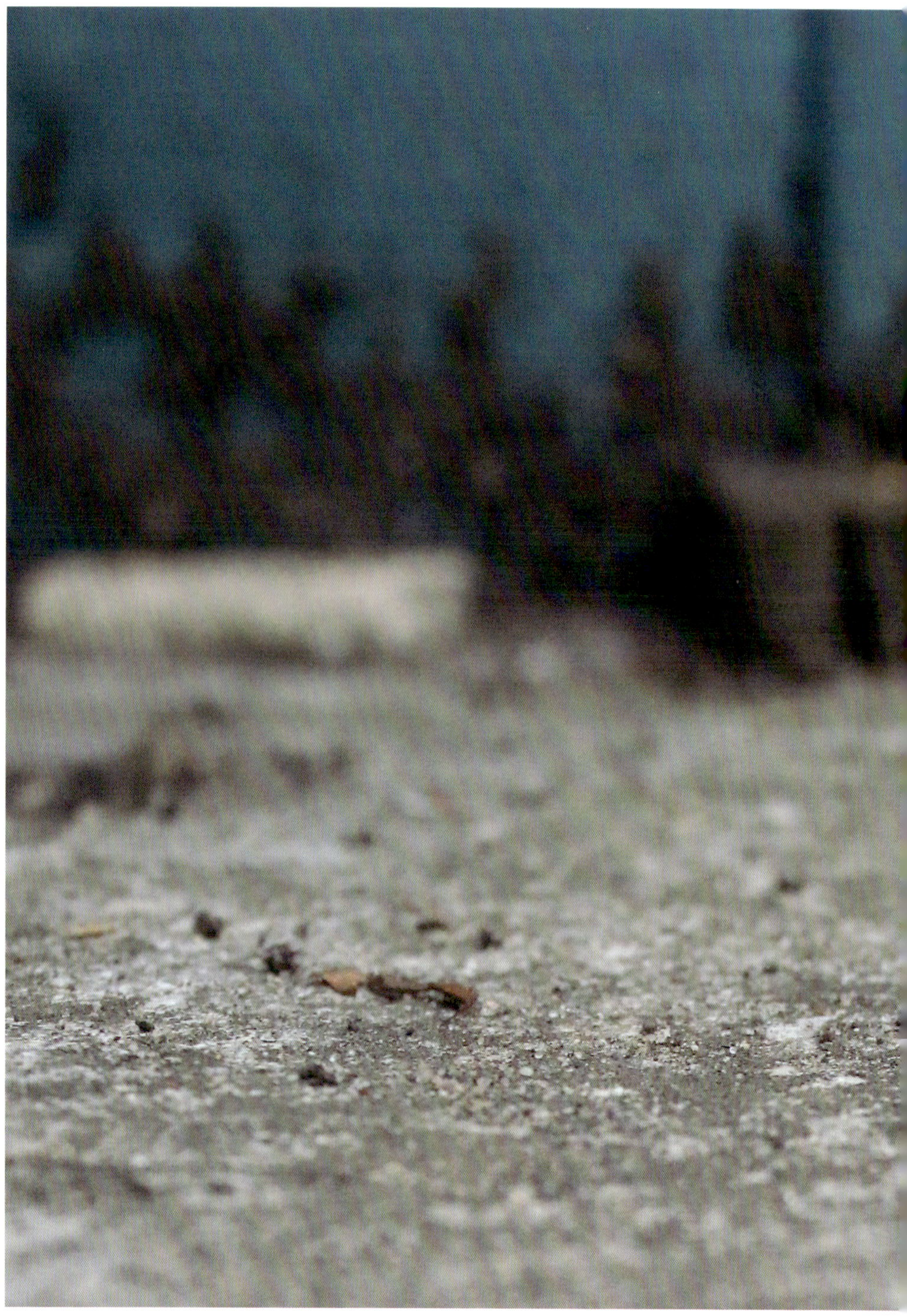

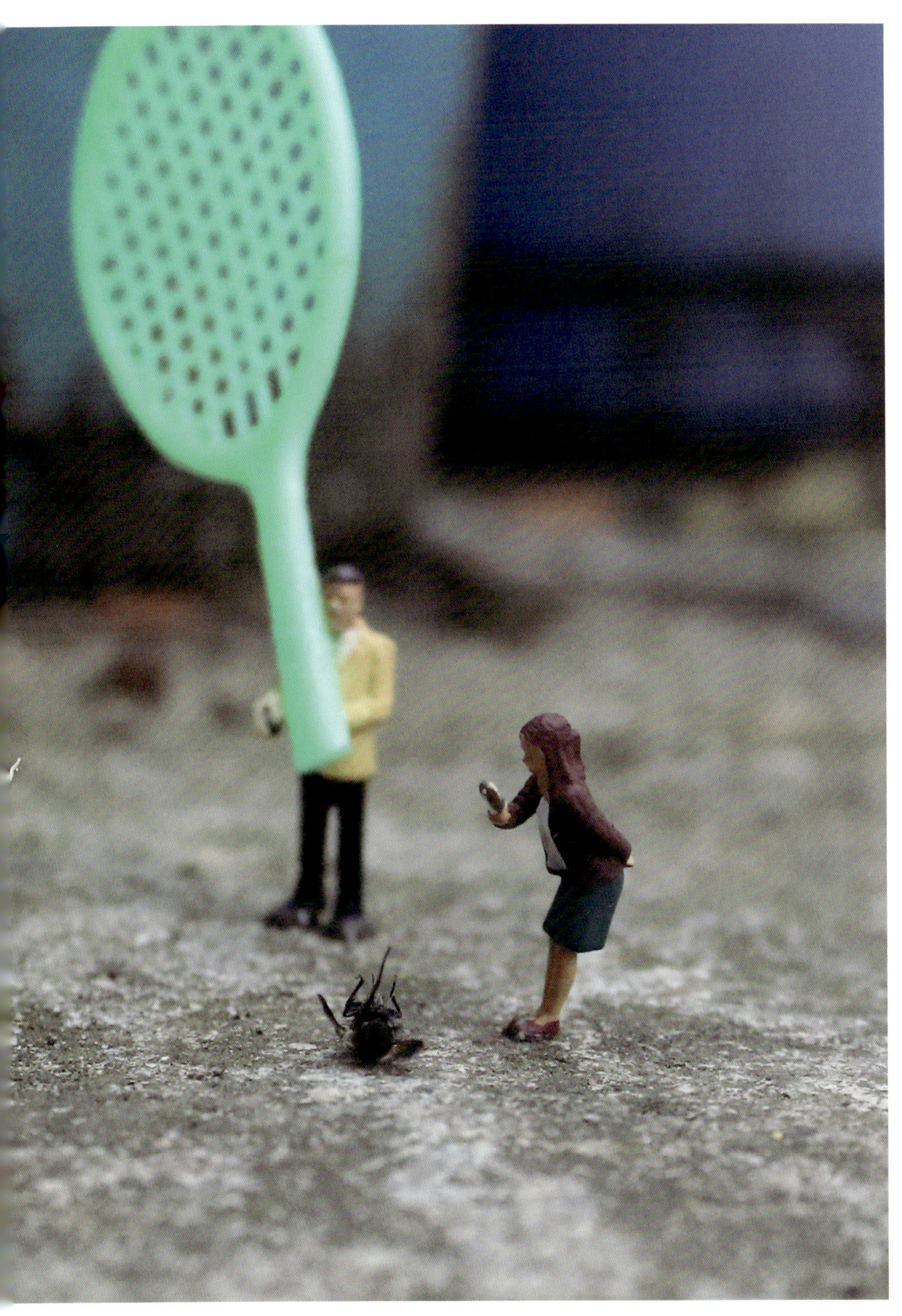

Mission Accomplished!

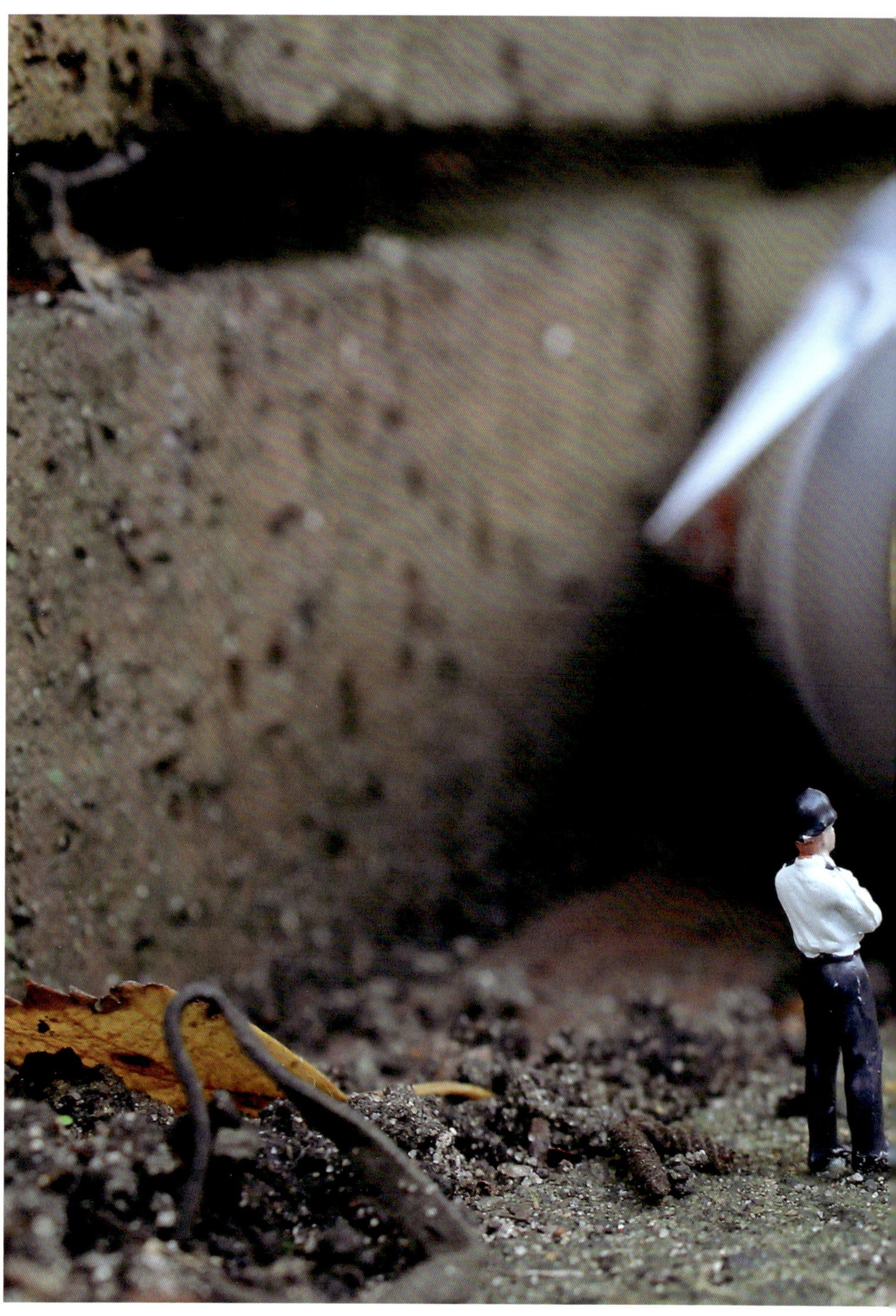

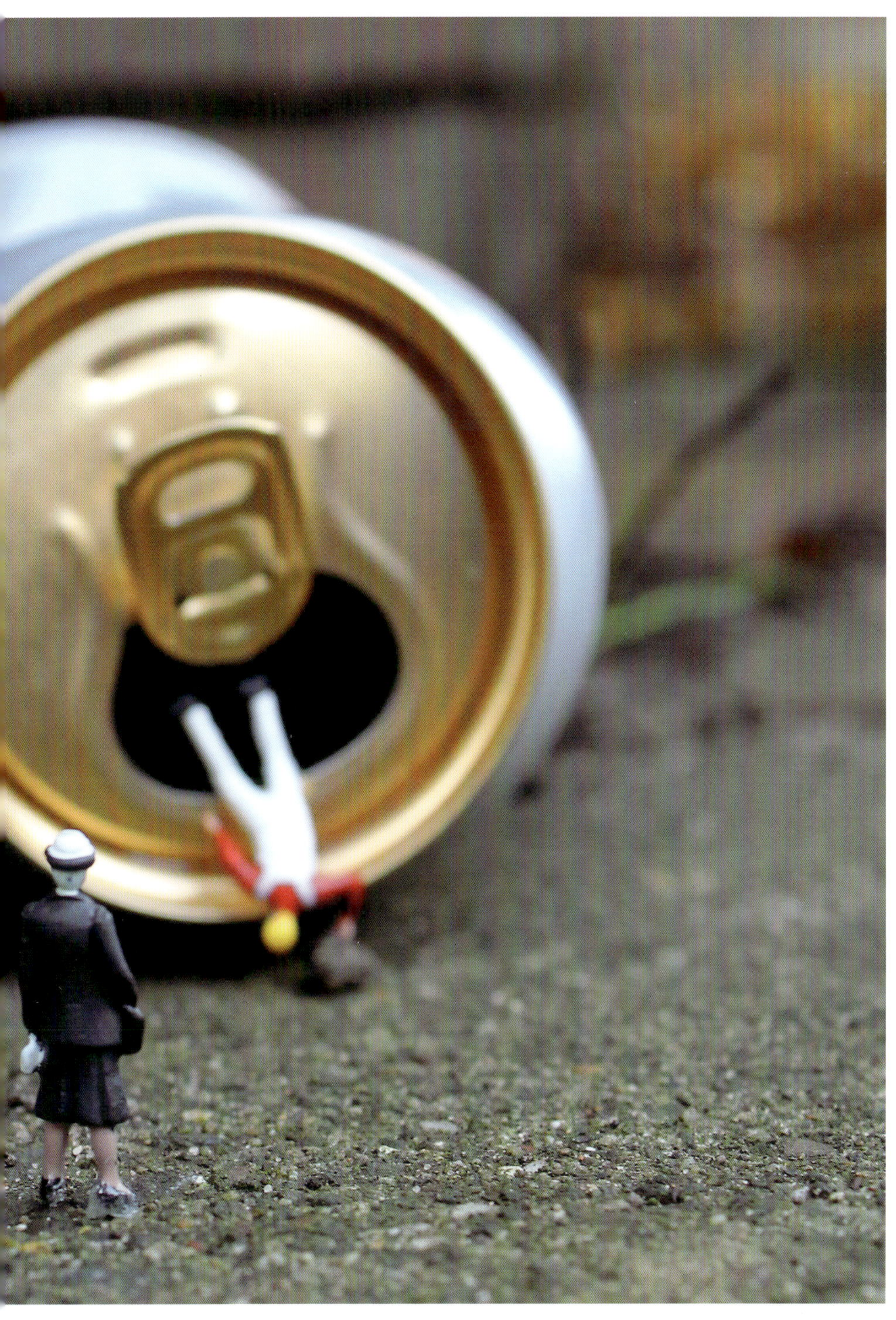

But I'm a Celebrity!

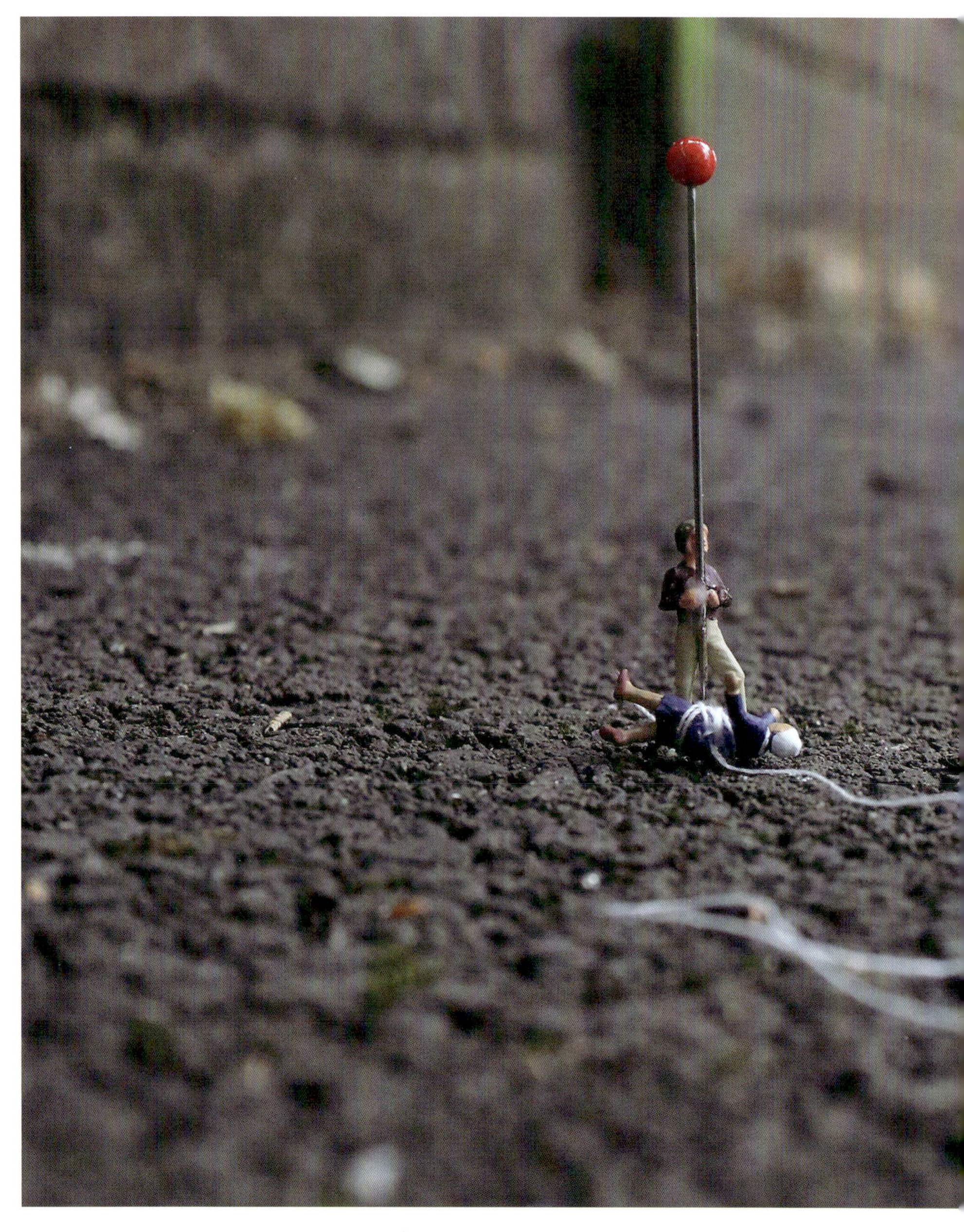

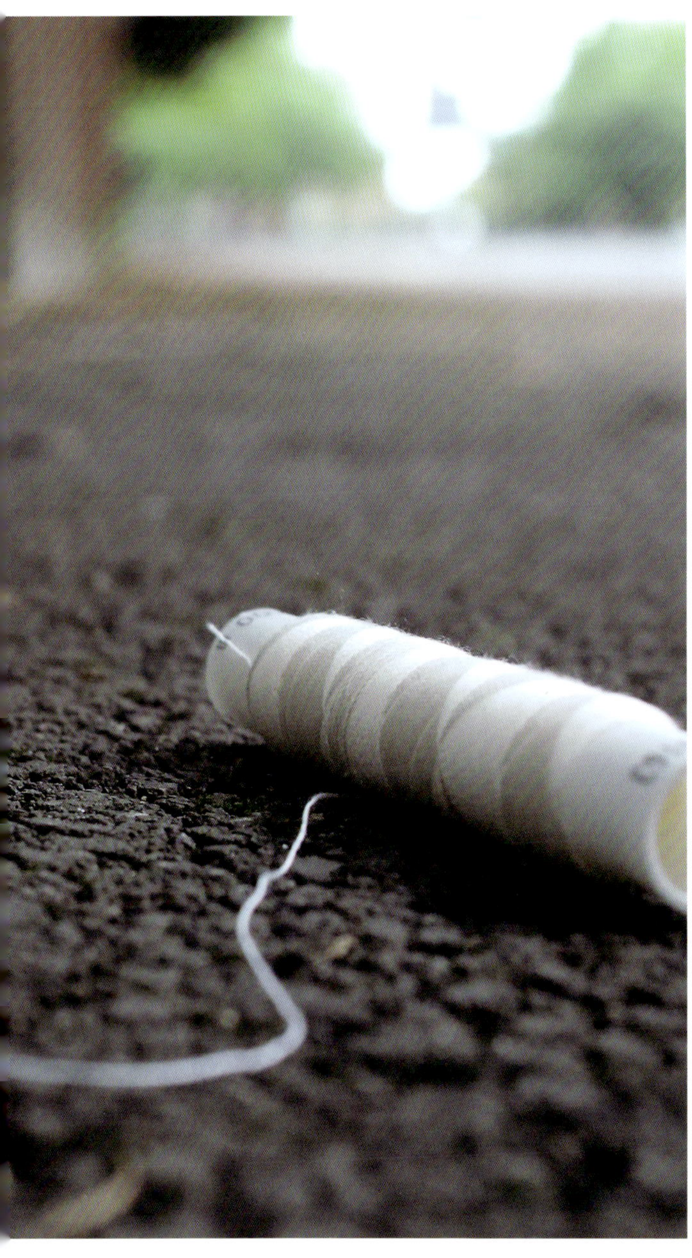

Pinned Down

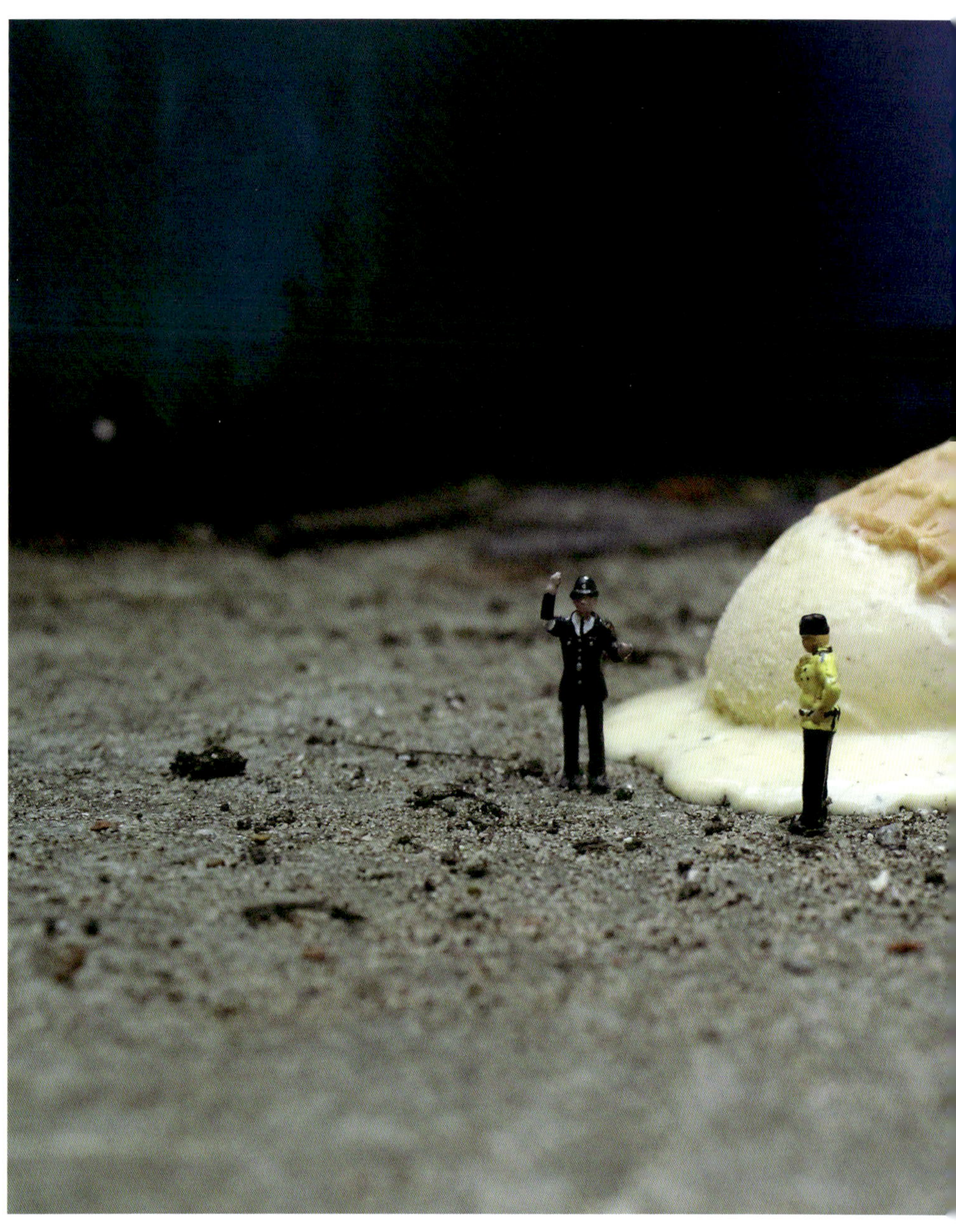

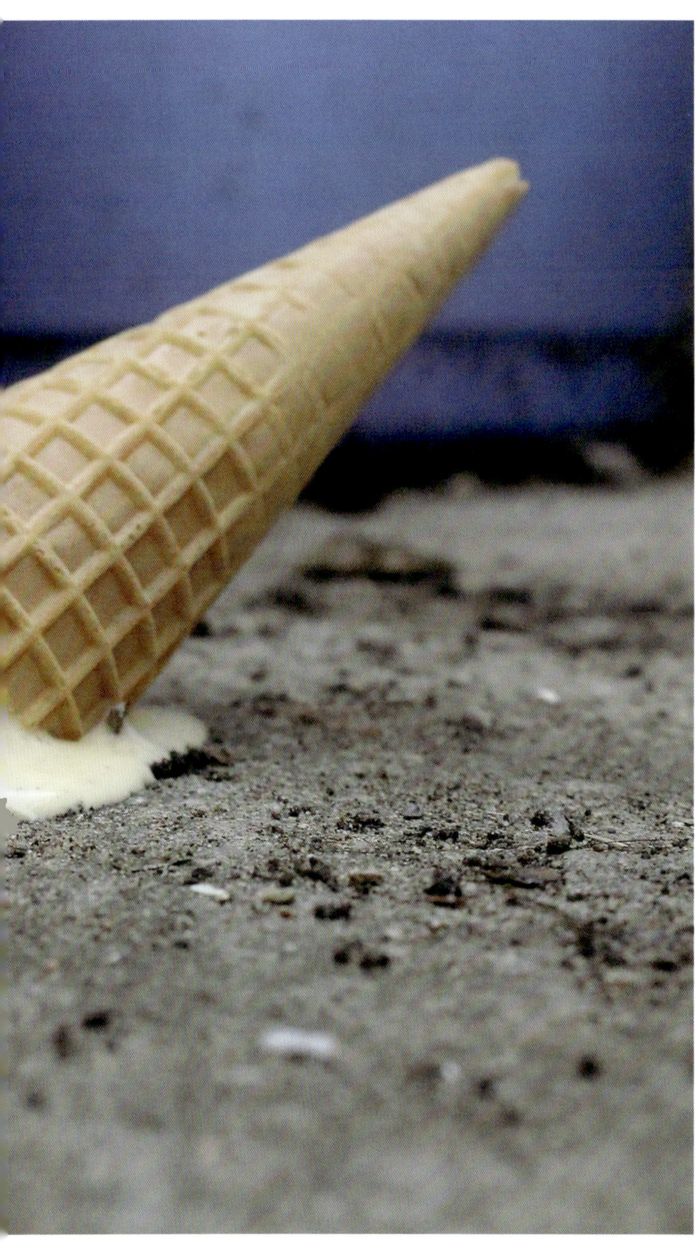

Ice Crime Scene

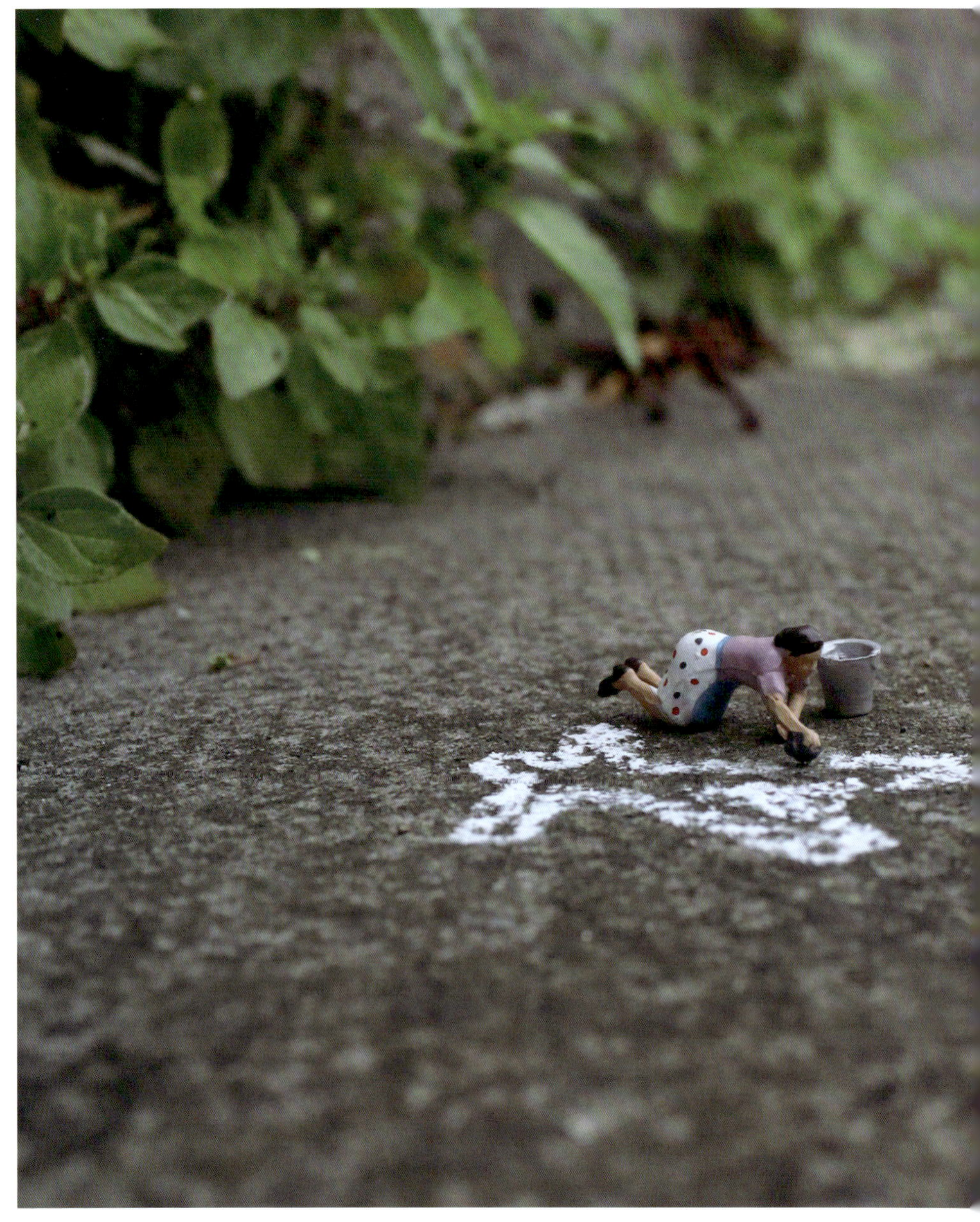

Nothing to See Here

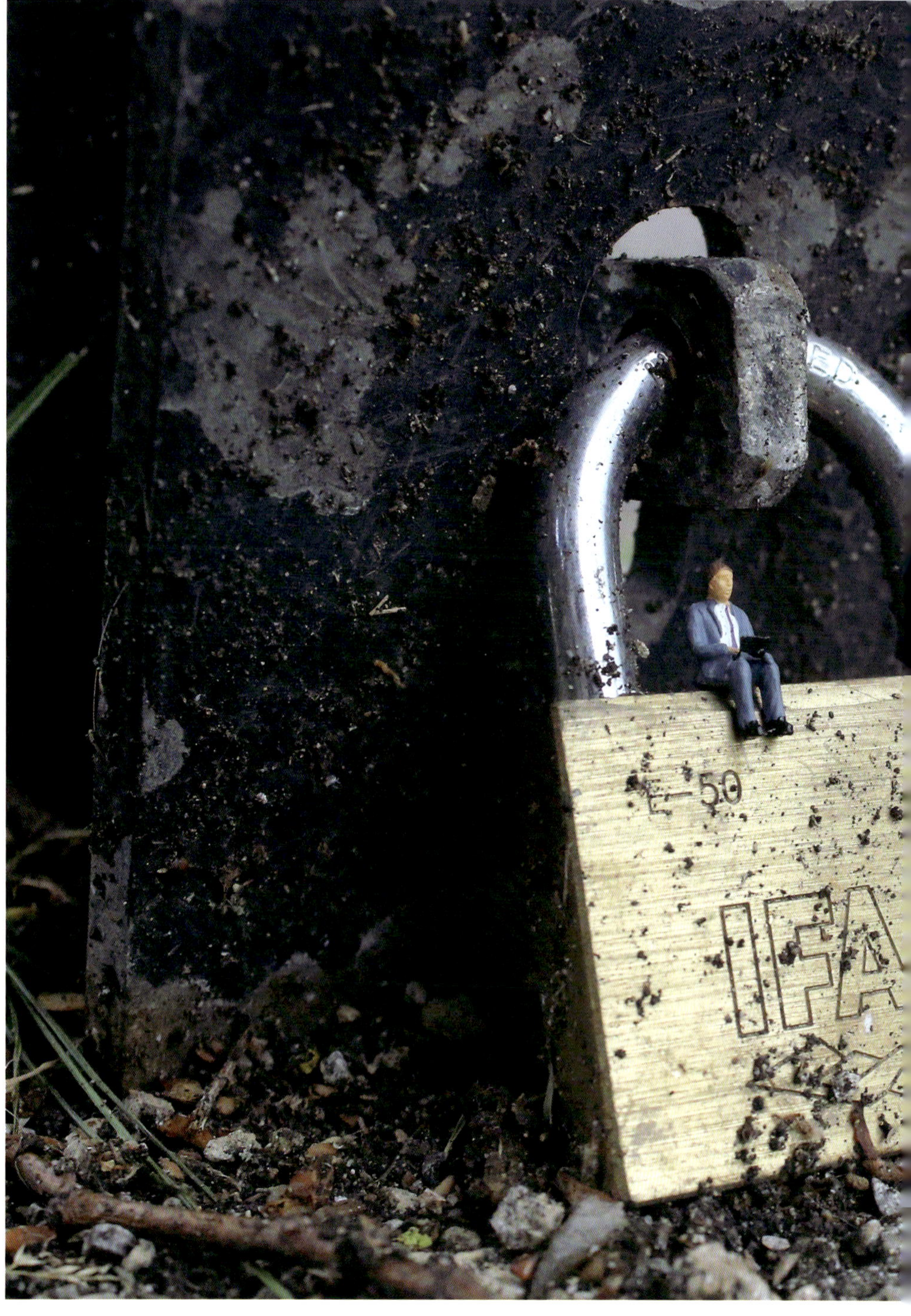
50
IFA

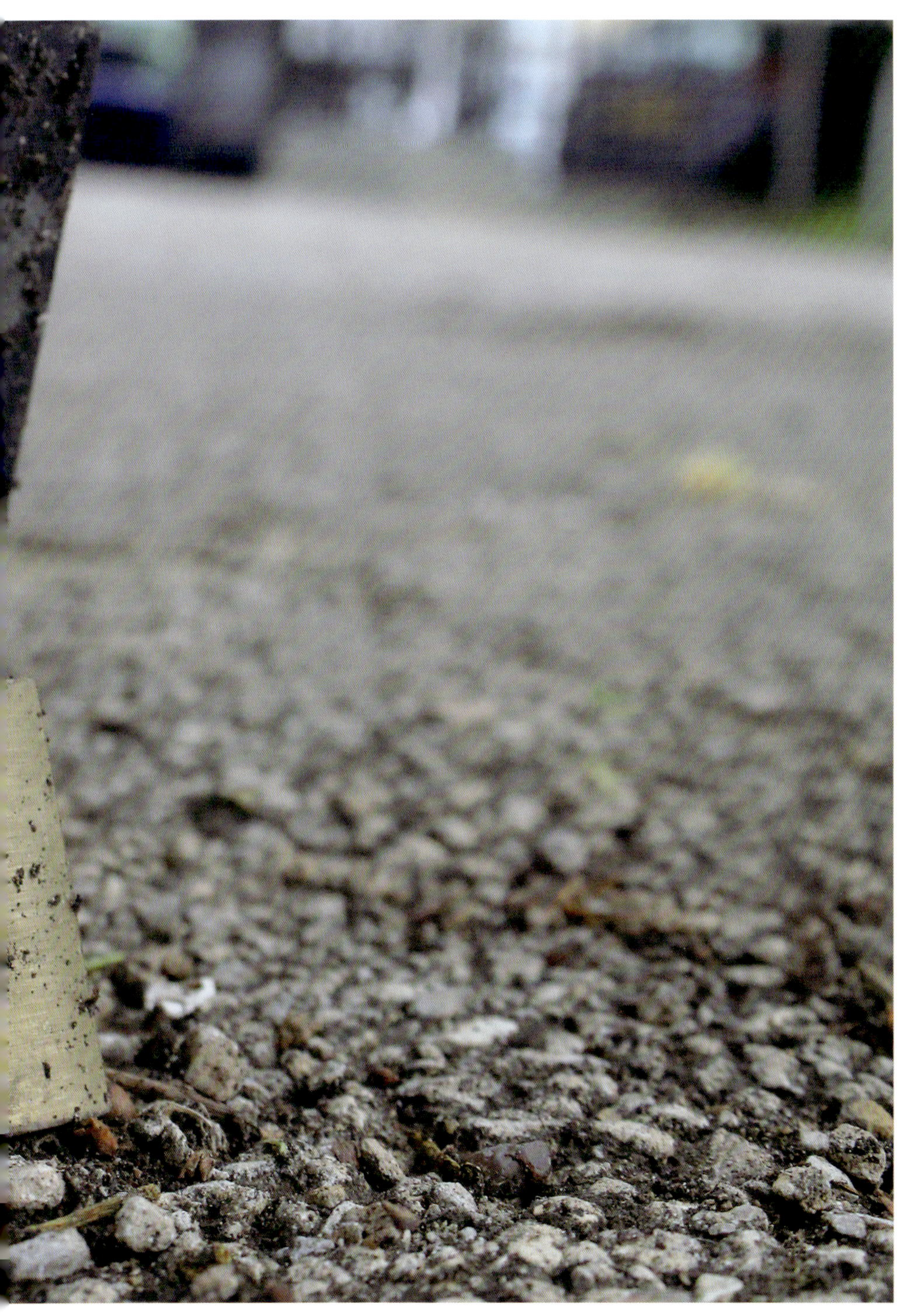

Laptop Security

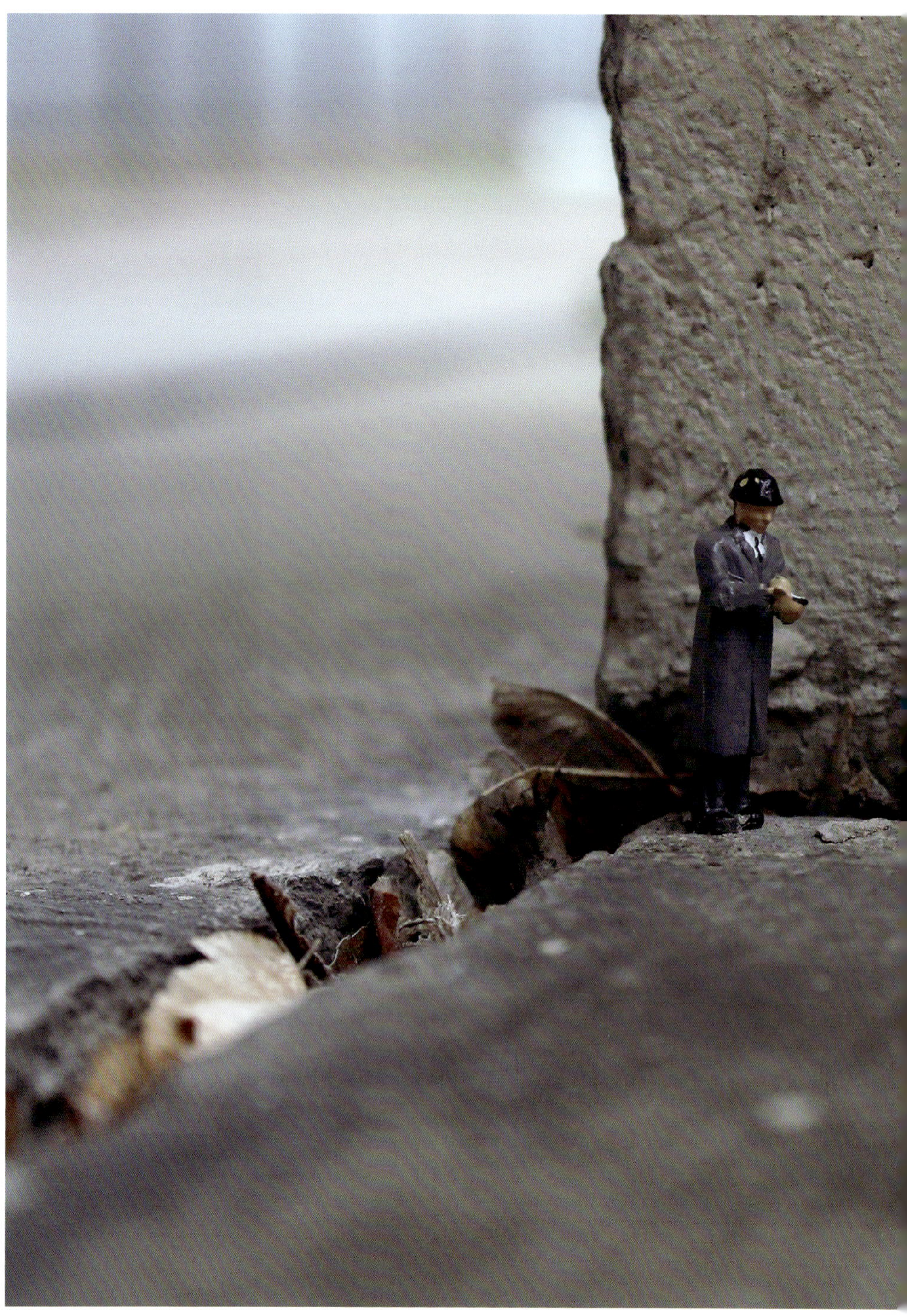

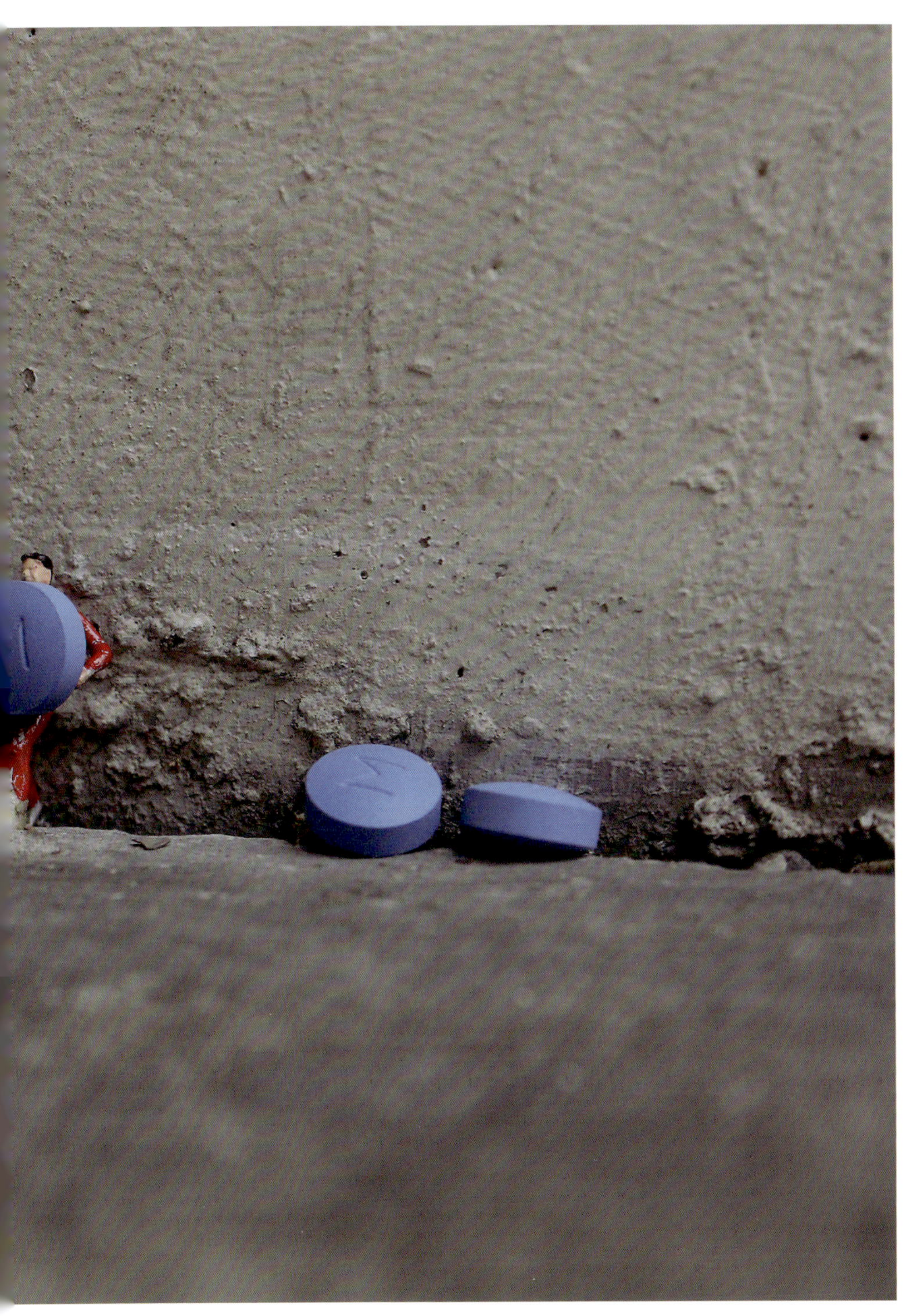

It's Only Three ****ing Pills!

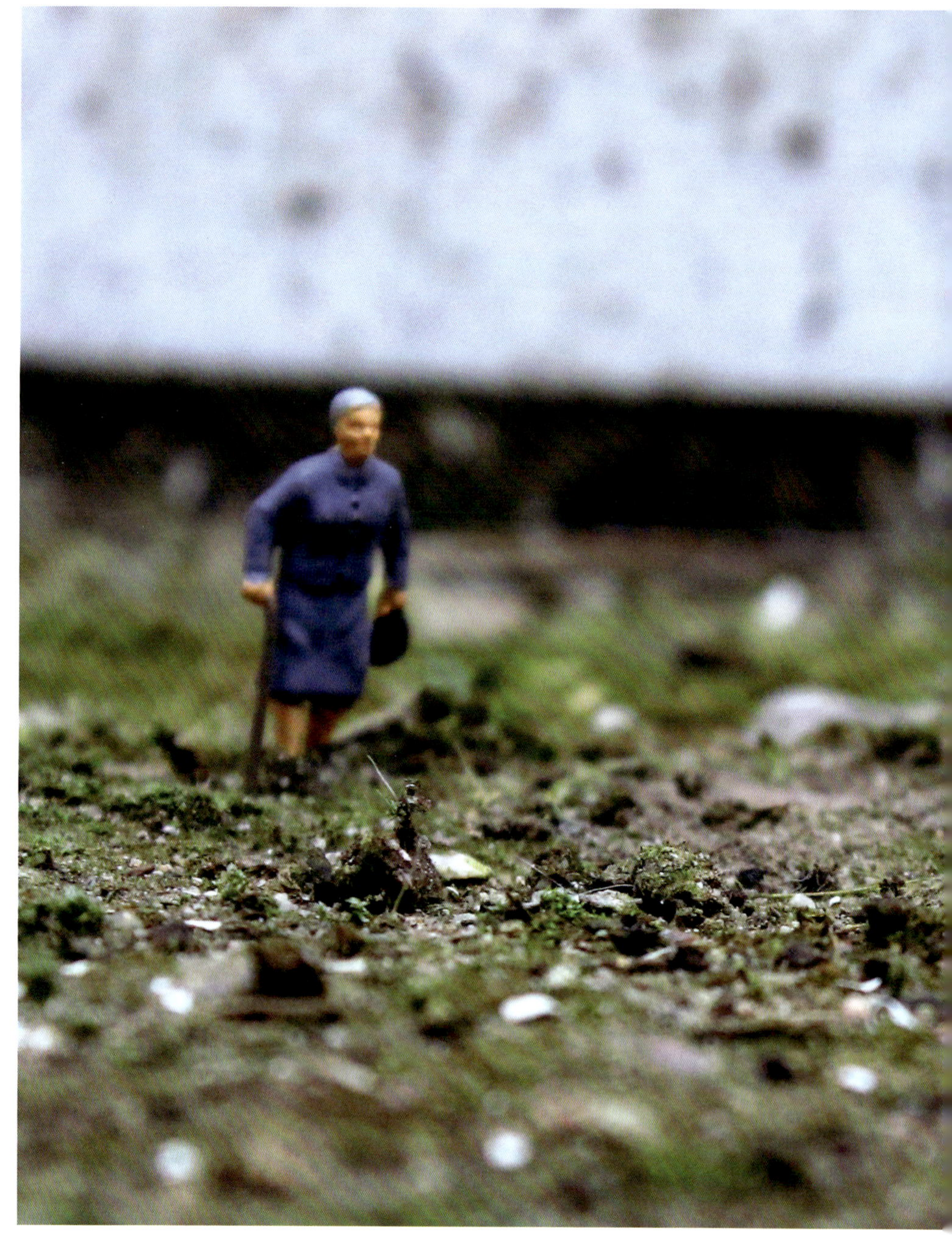

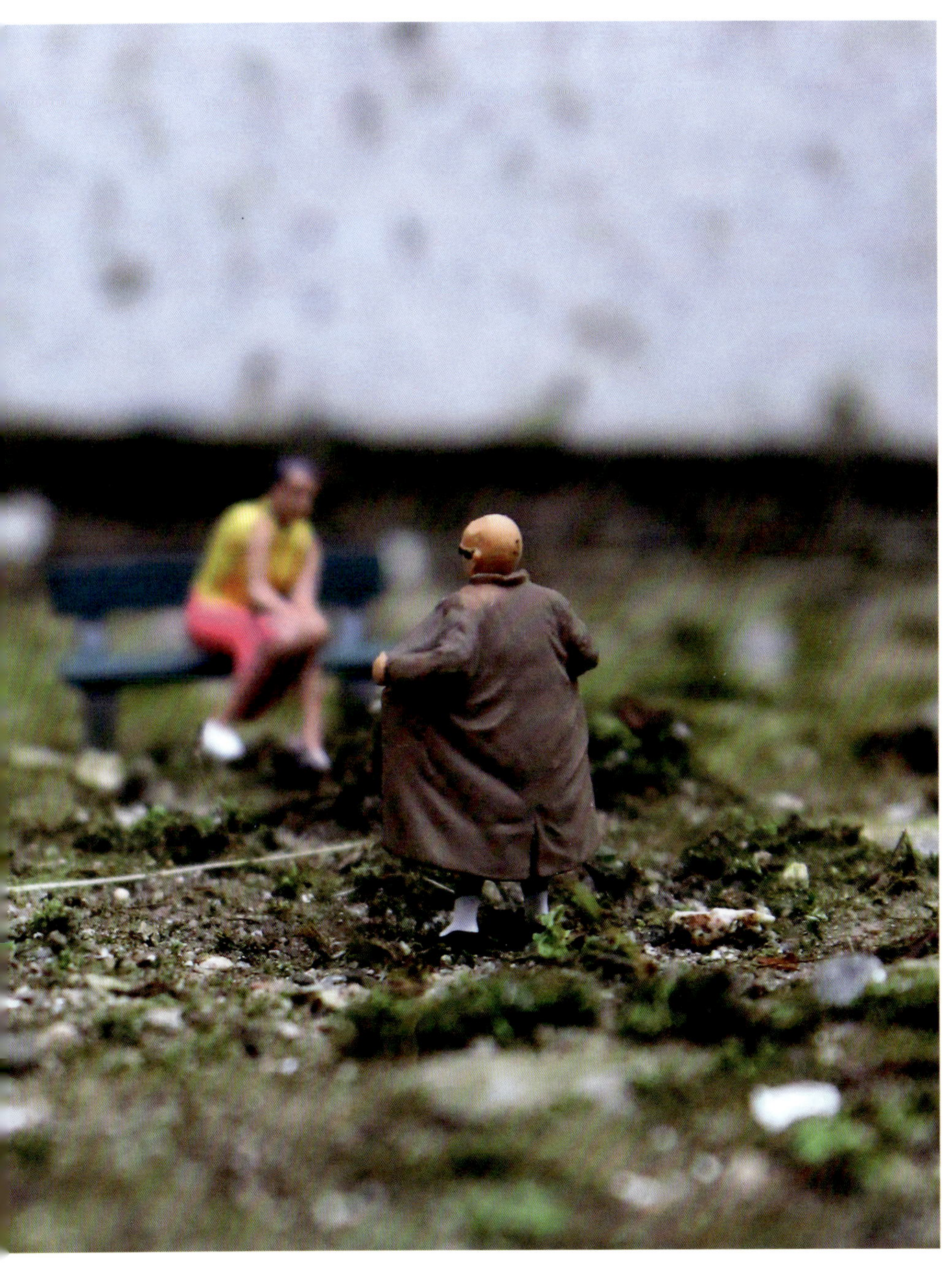

Indecent Exposure

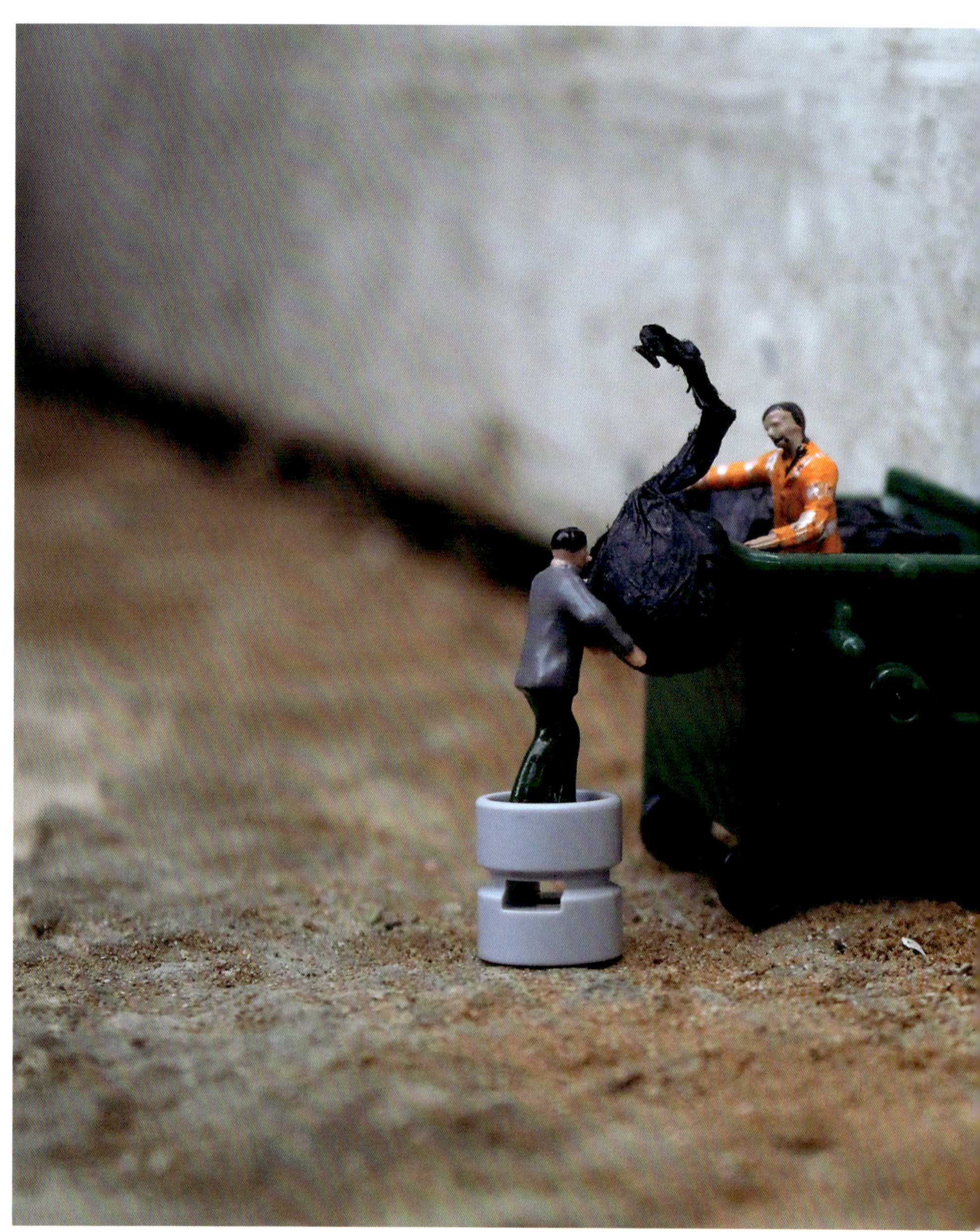

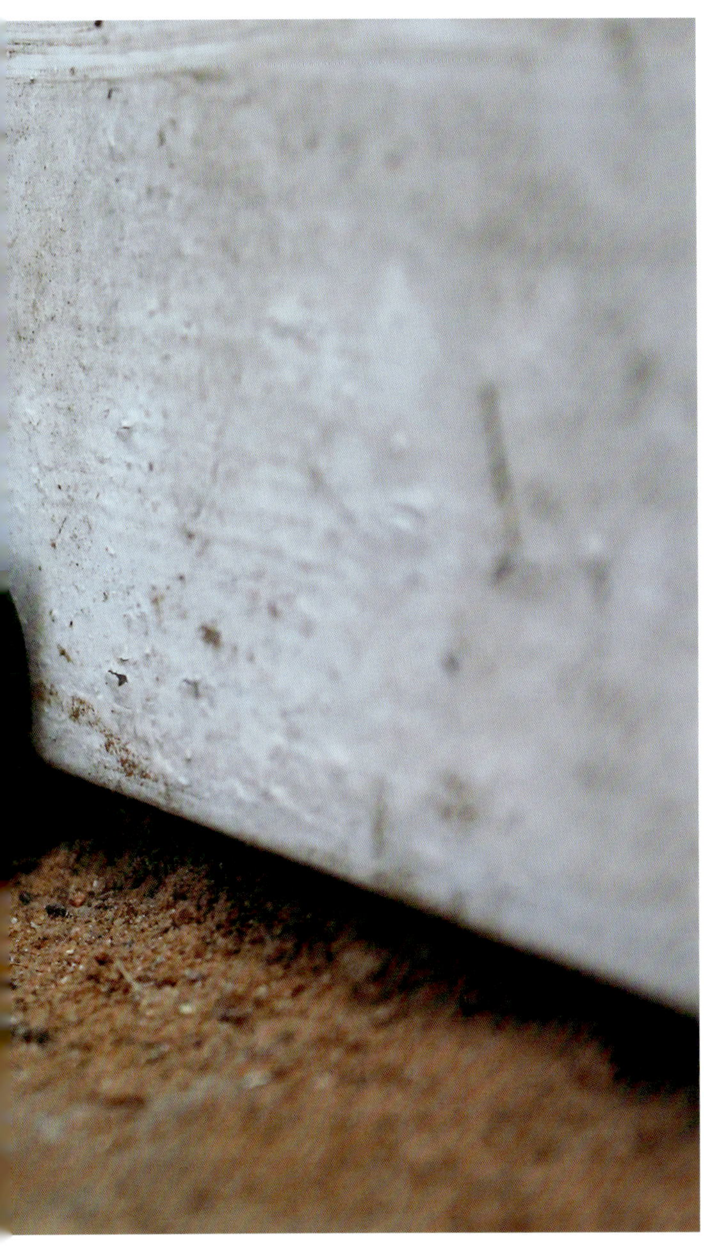

Austerity

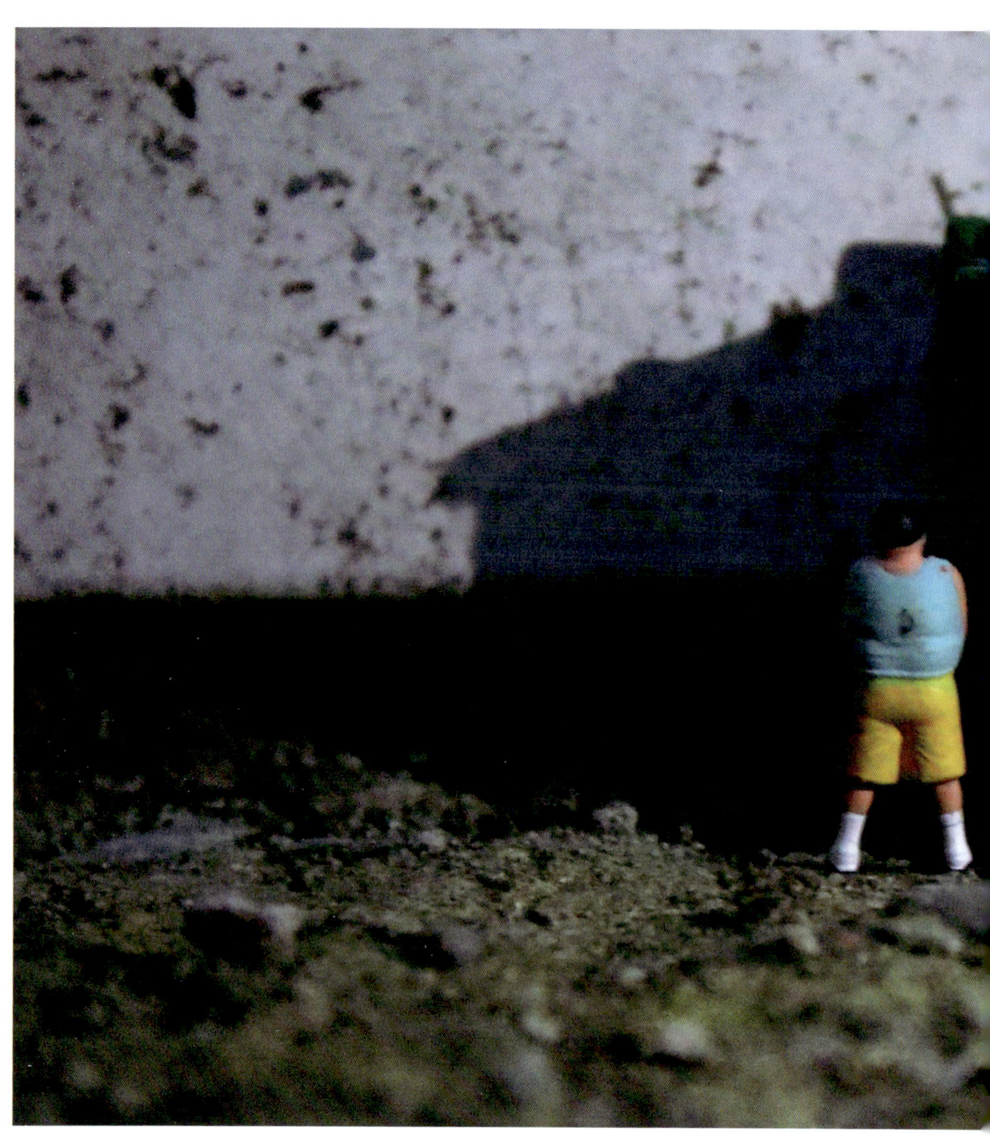

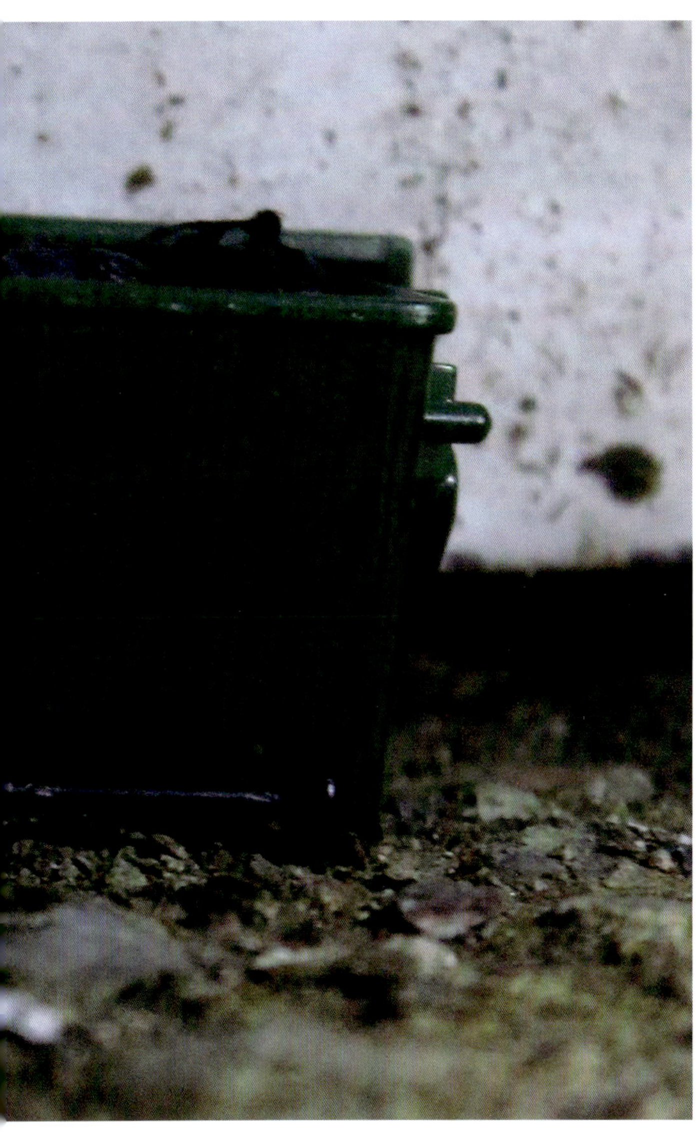

When You Have to Go

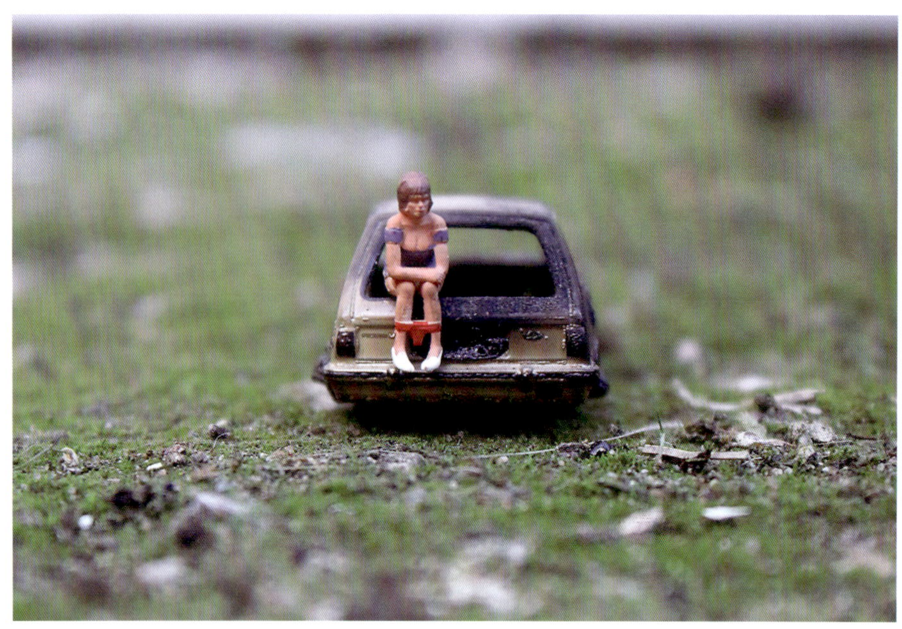

Outdoor Toilet i

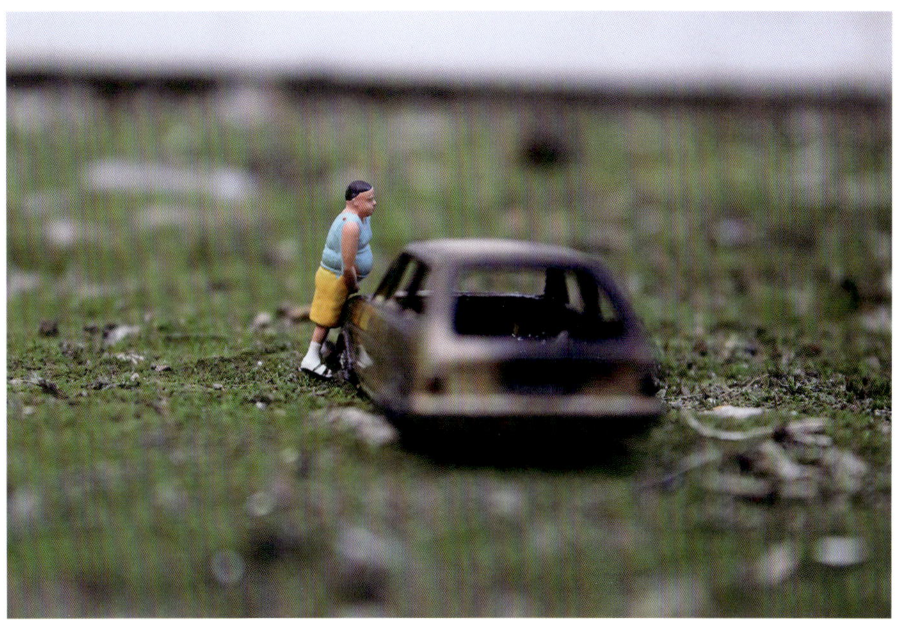

Outdoor Toilet ii

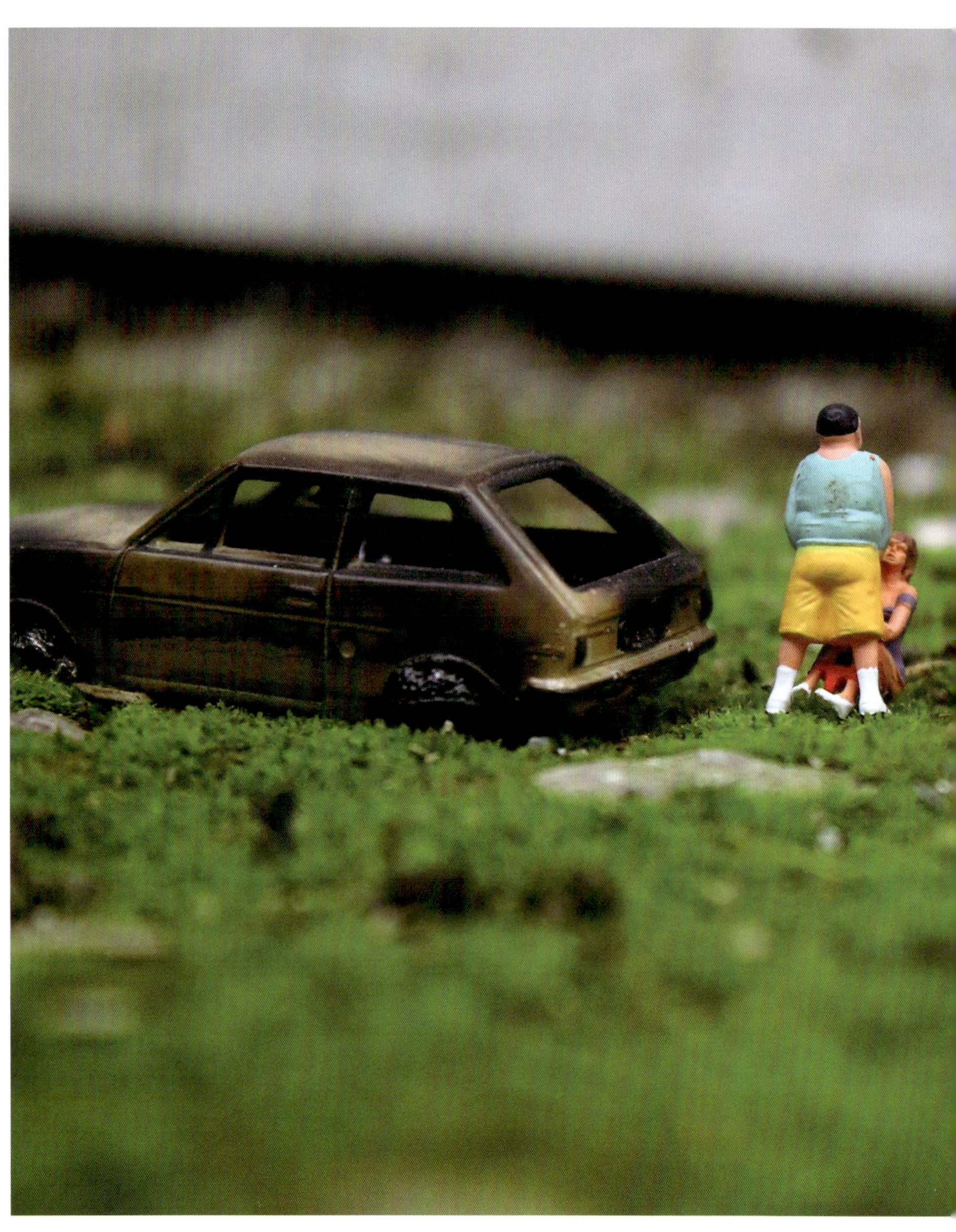

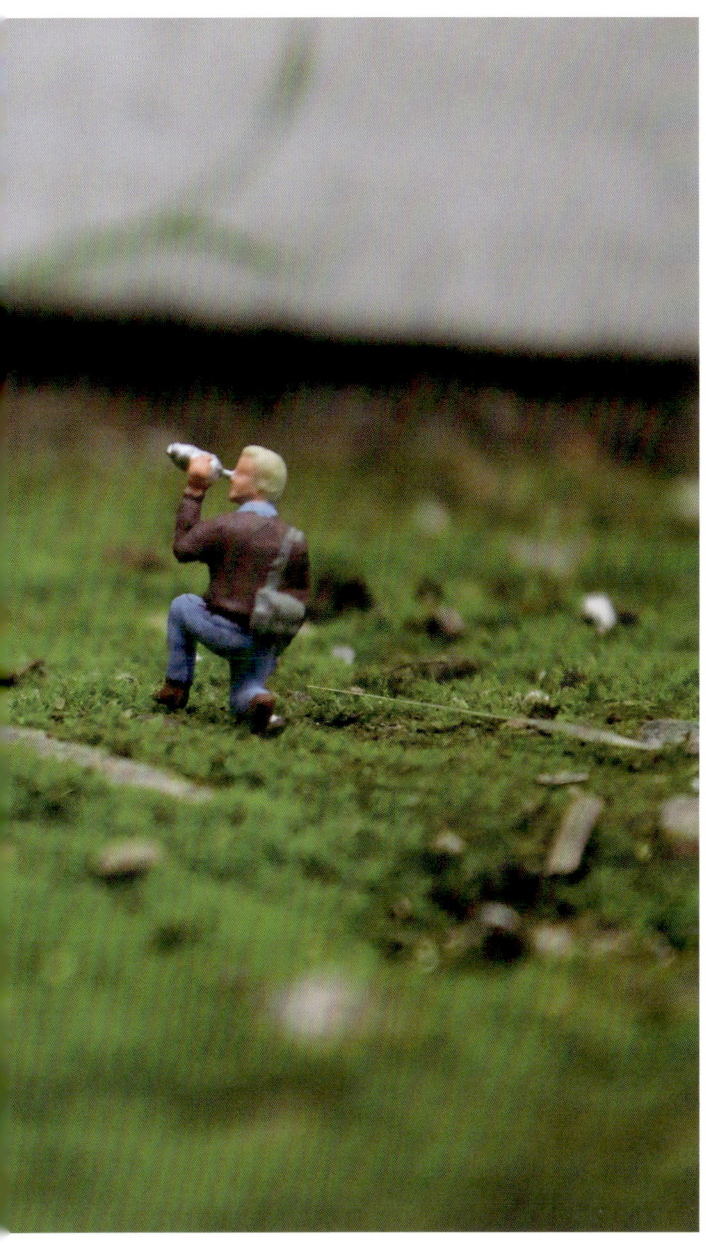

One for the Road

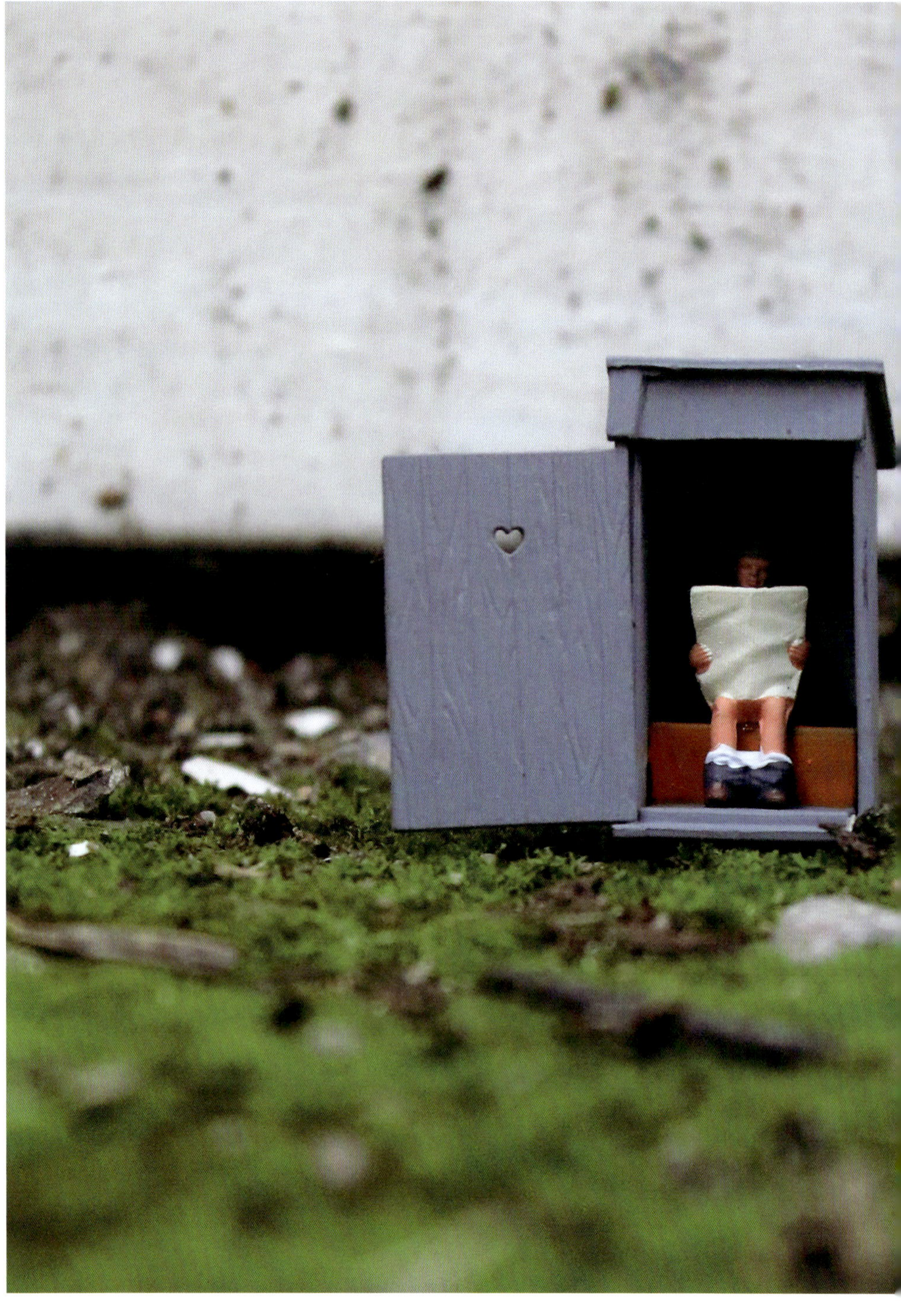

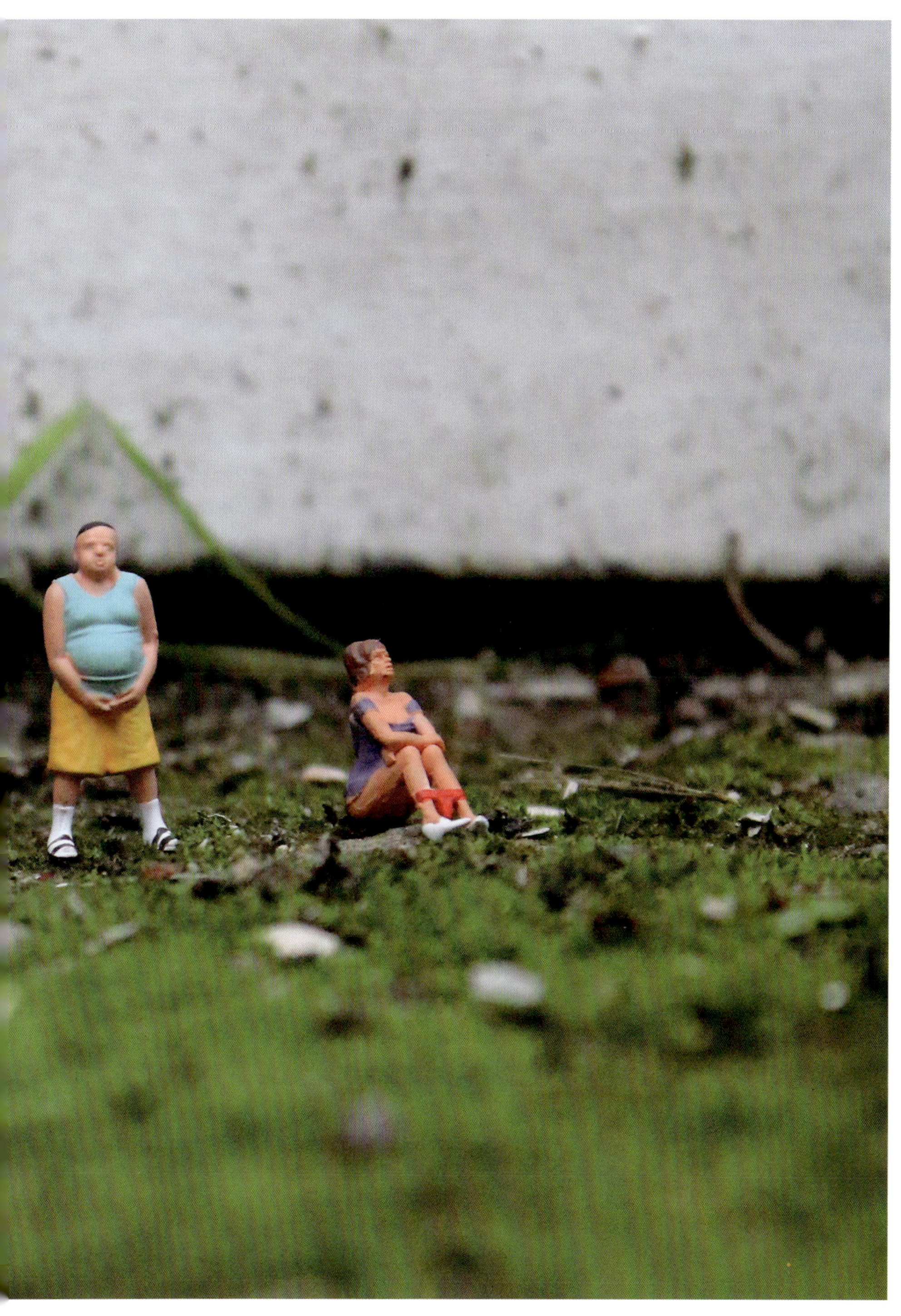

Waiting for the Loo

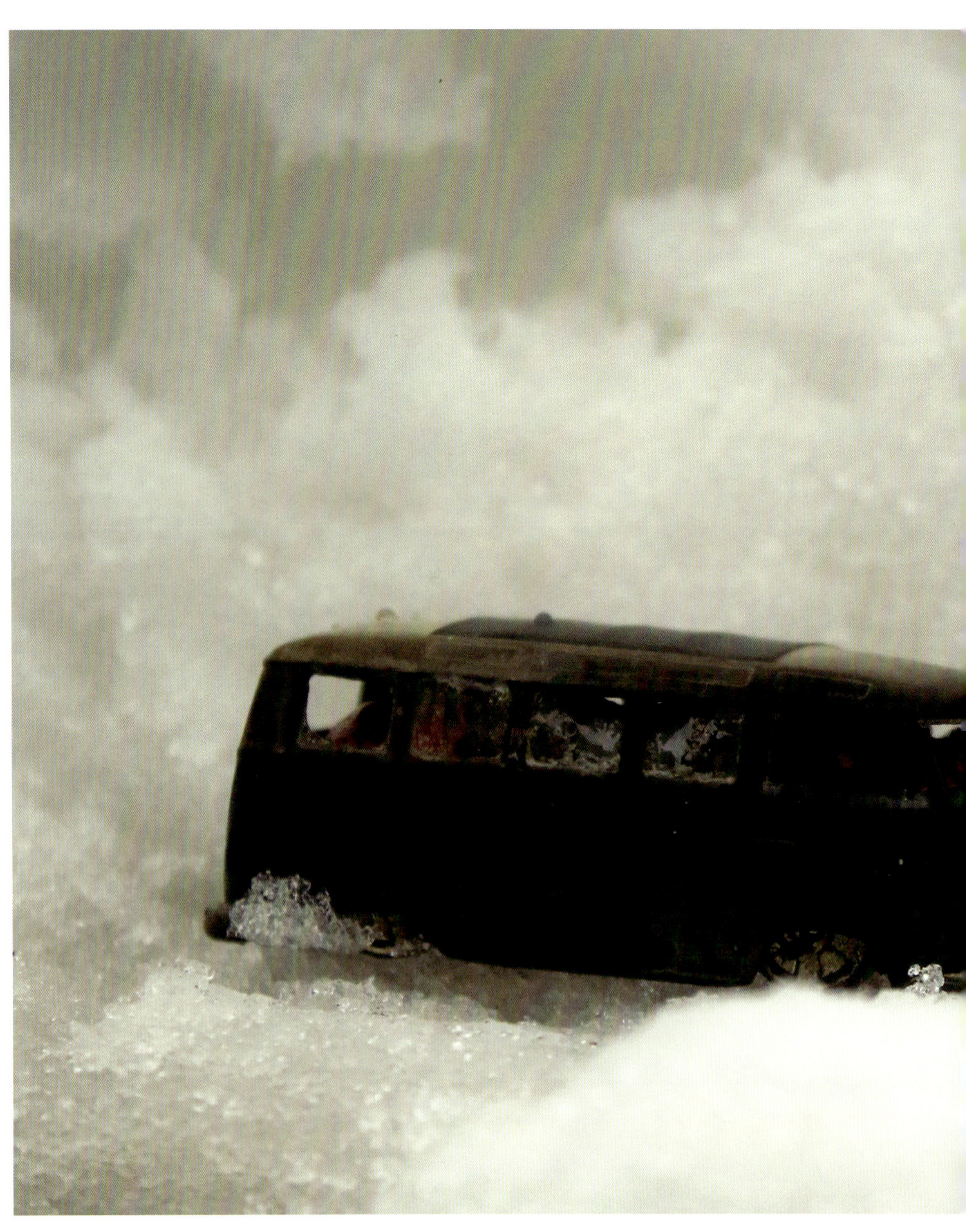

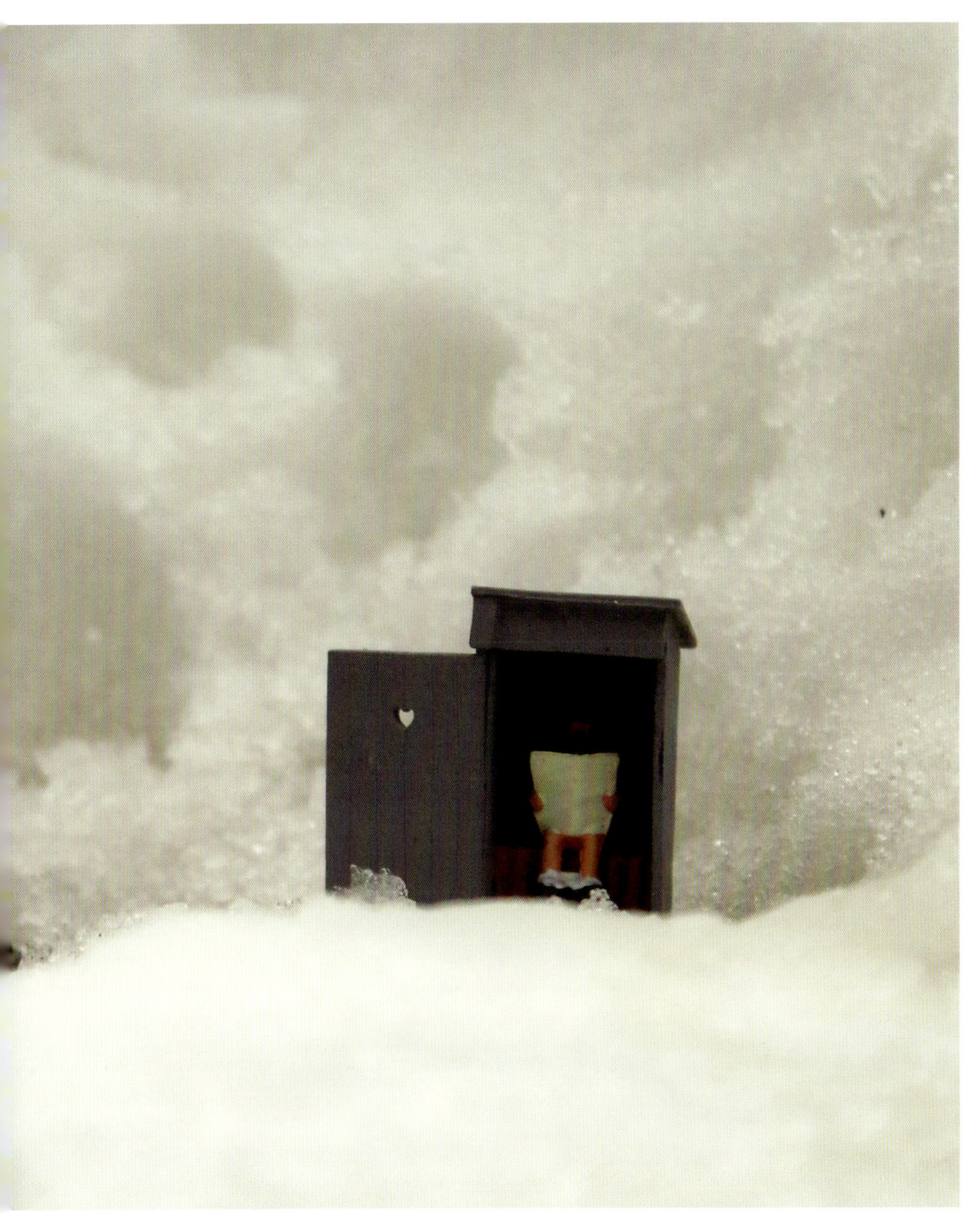

Dump Stop

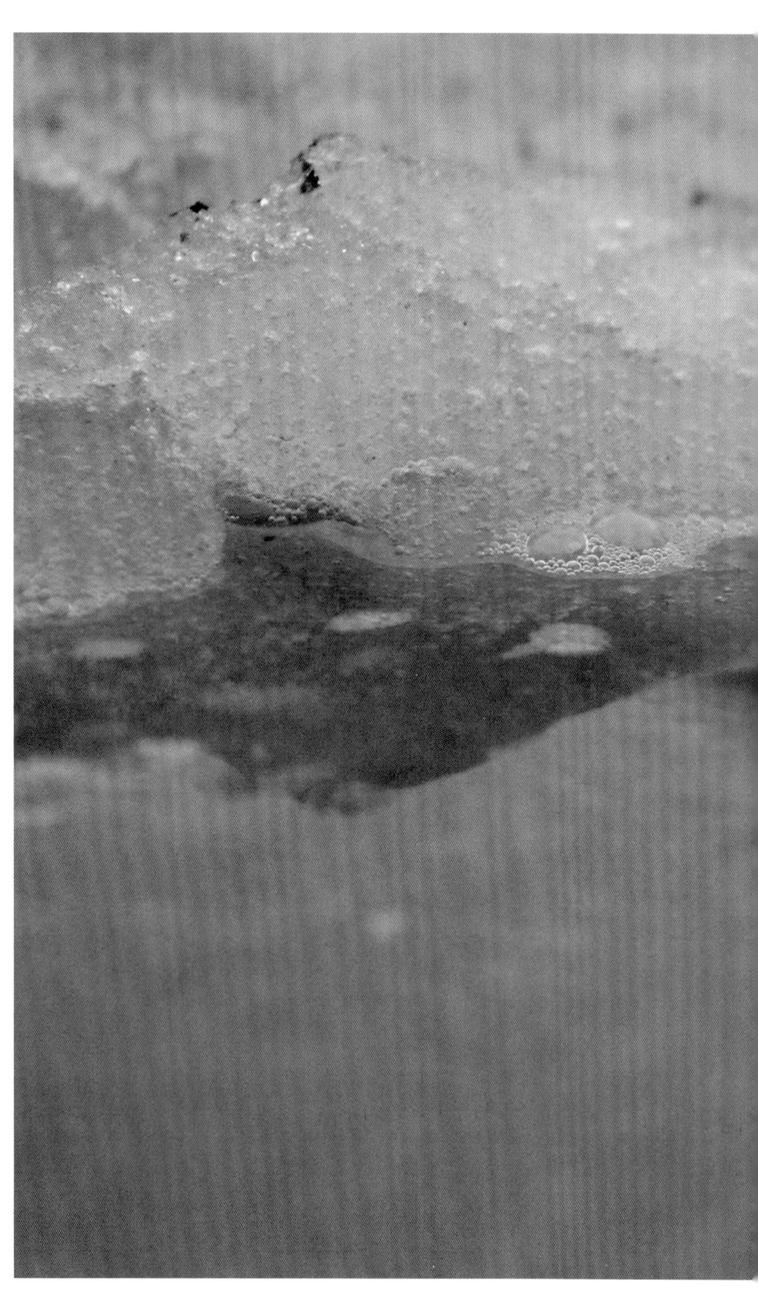

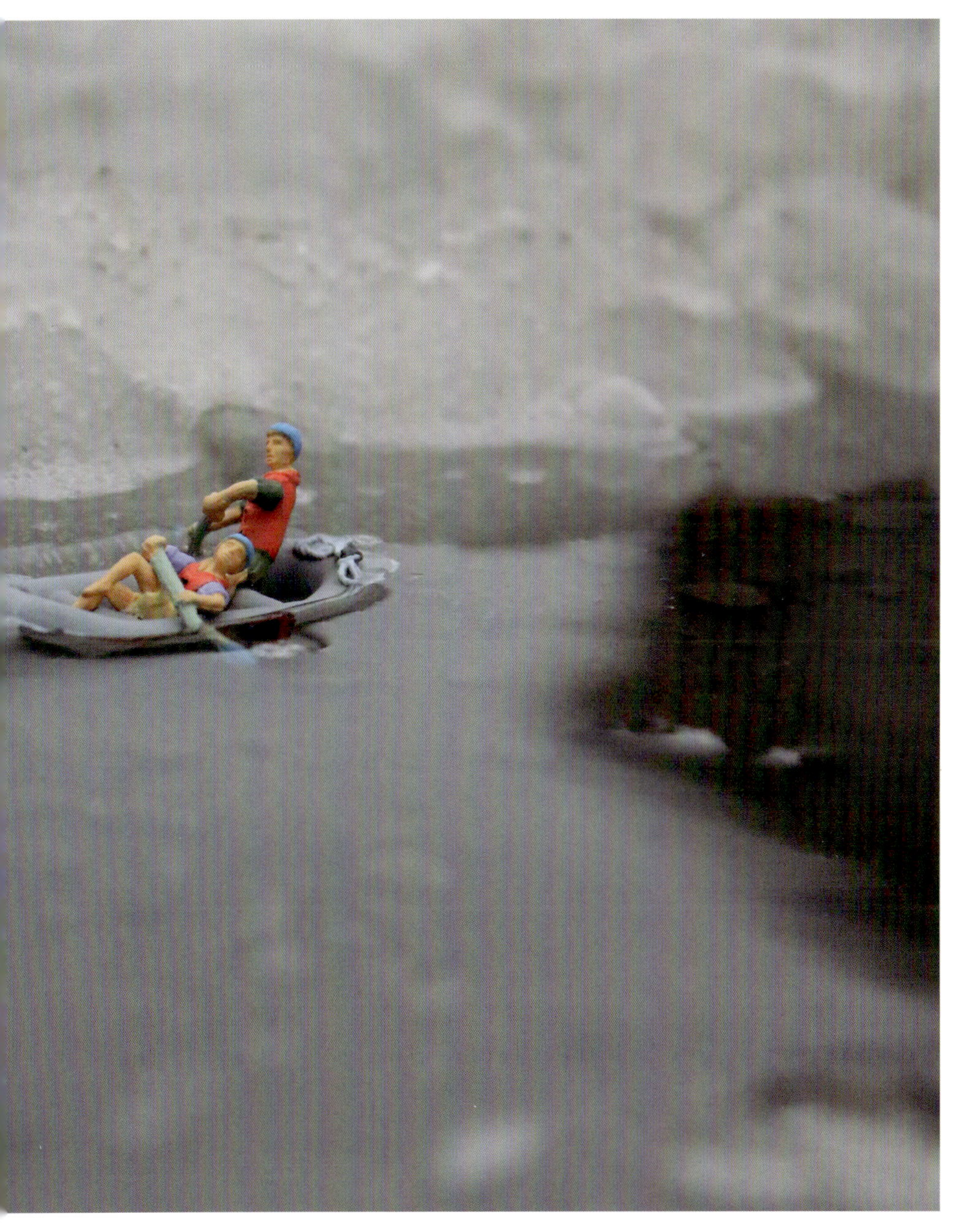

Ice Rafting

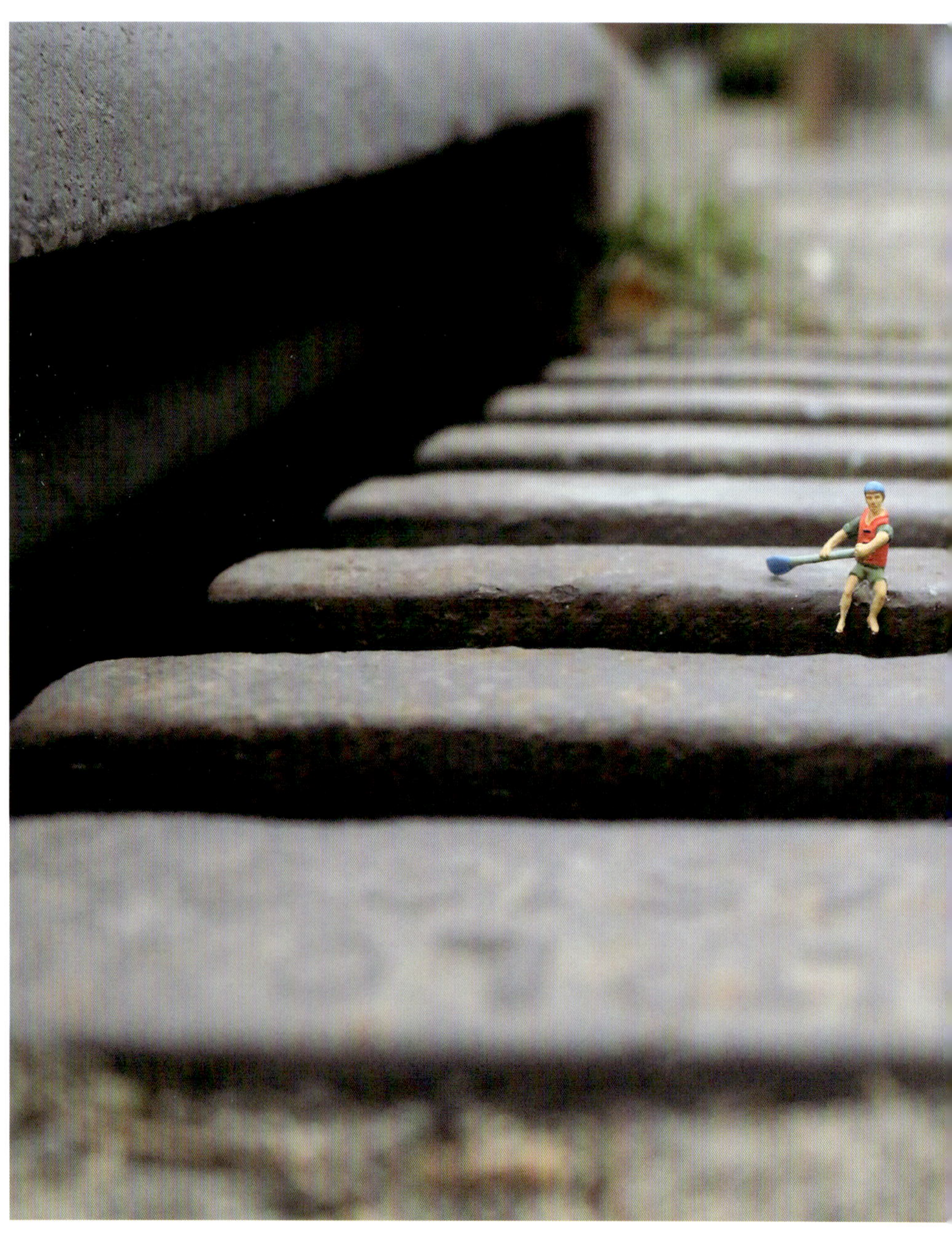

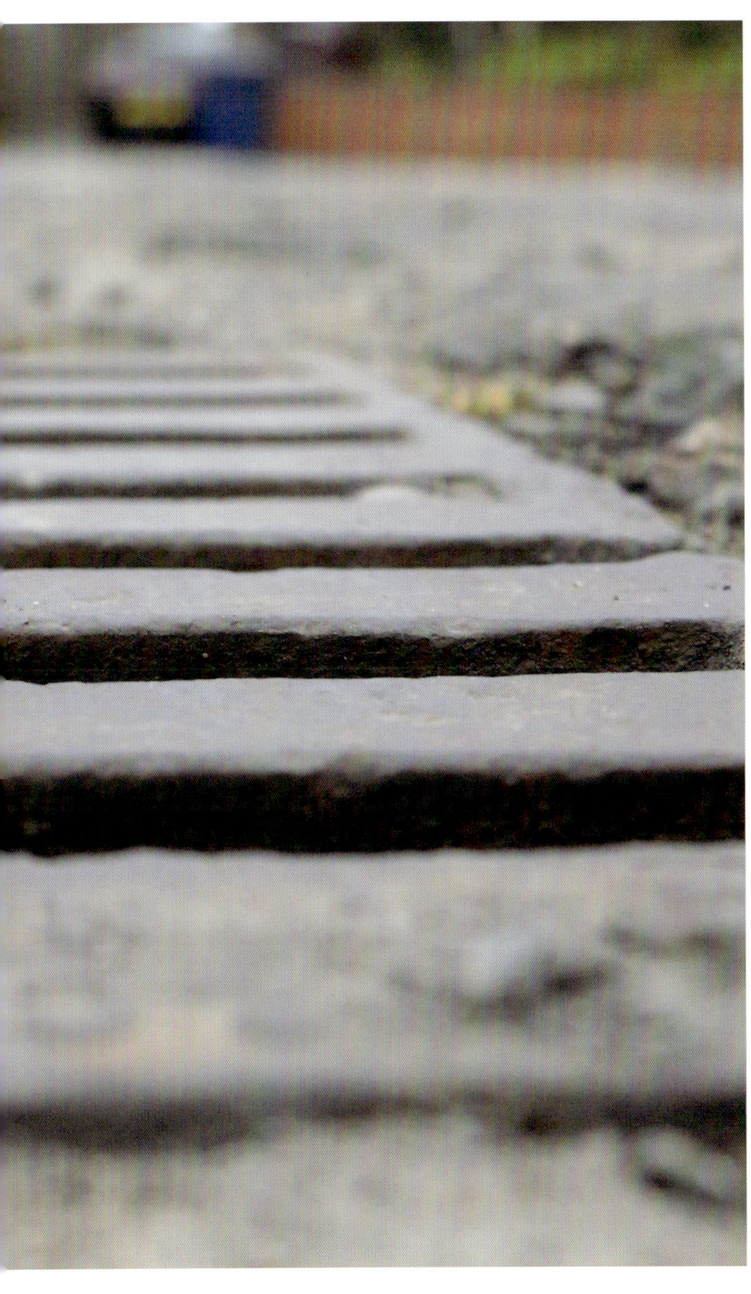

Urban Rafting

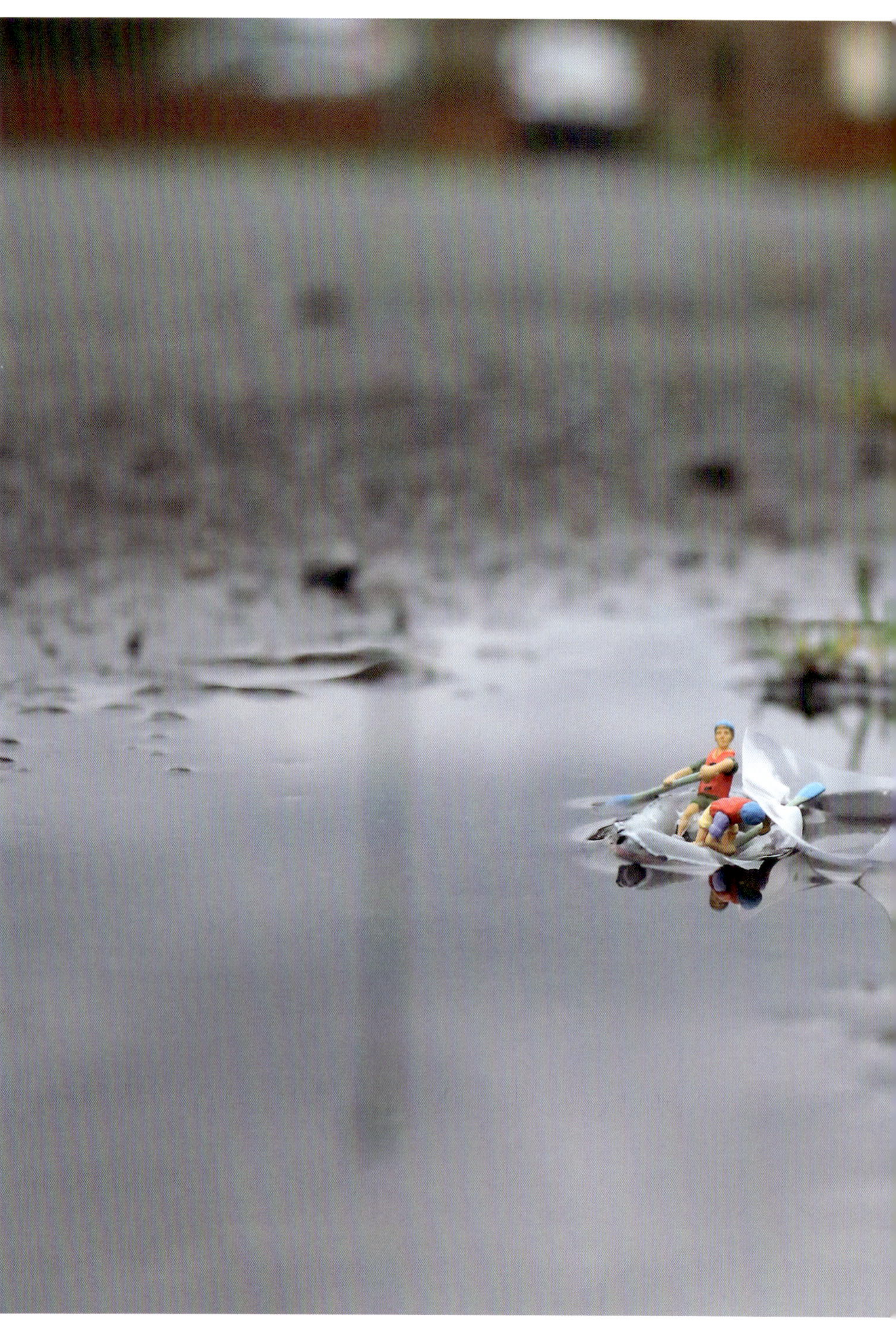

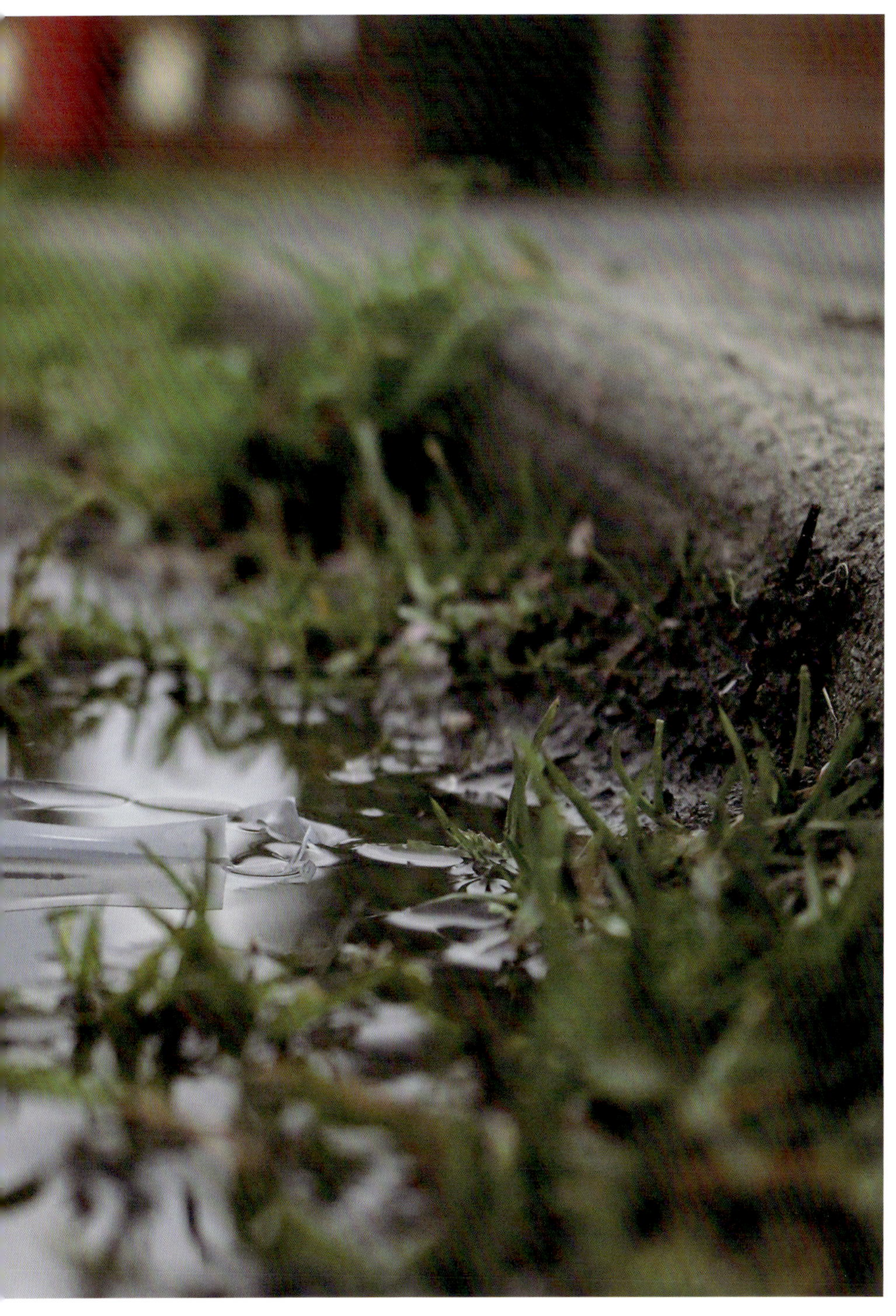

Raft Obstruction

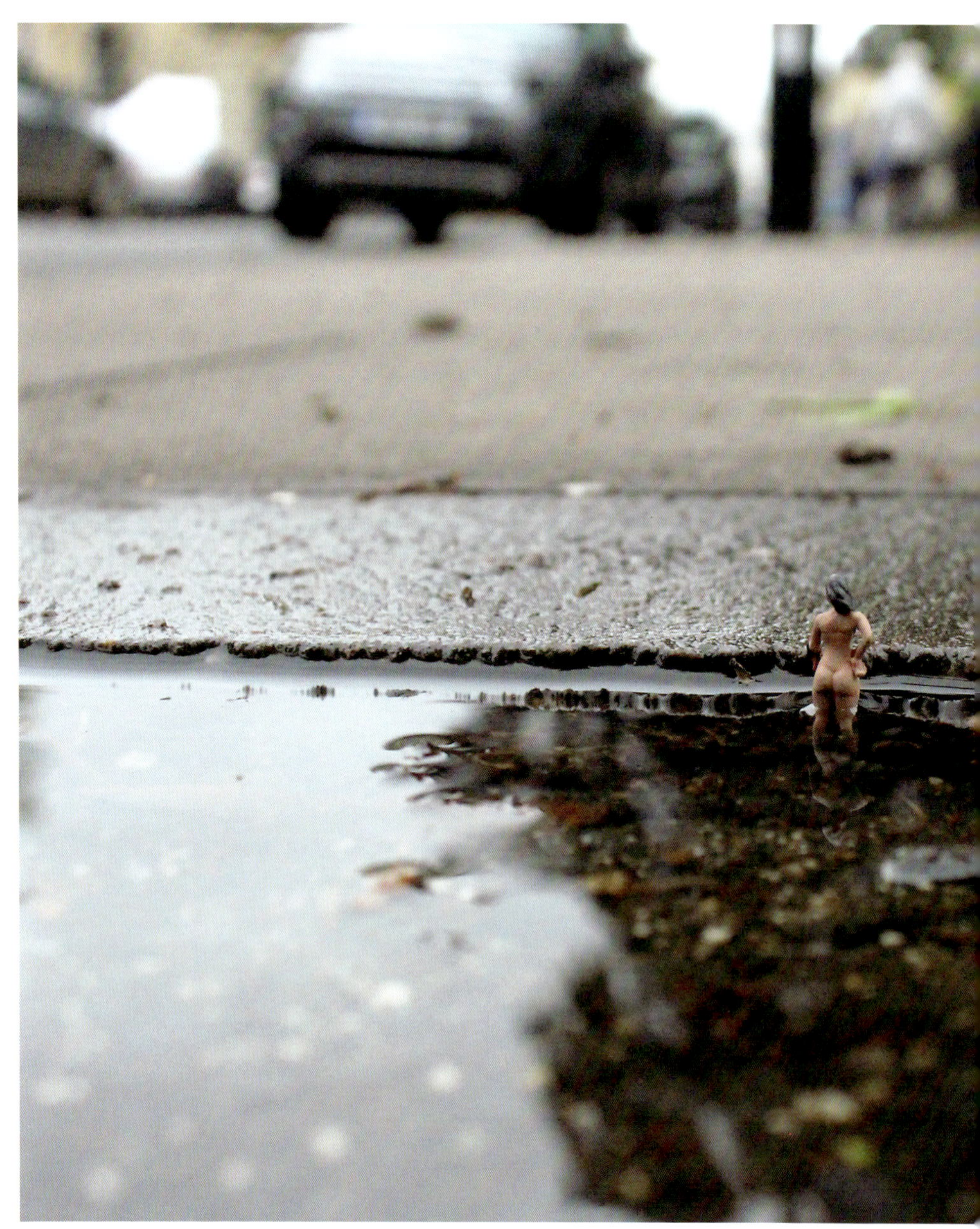

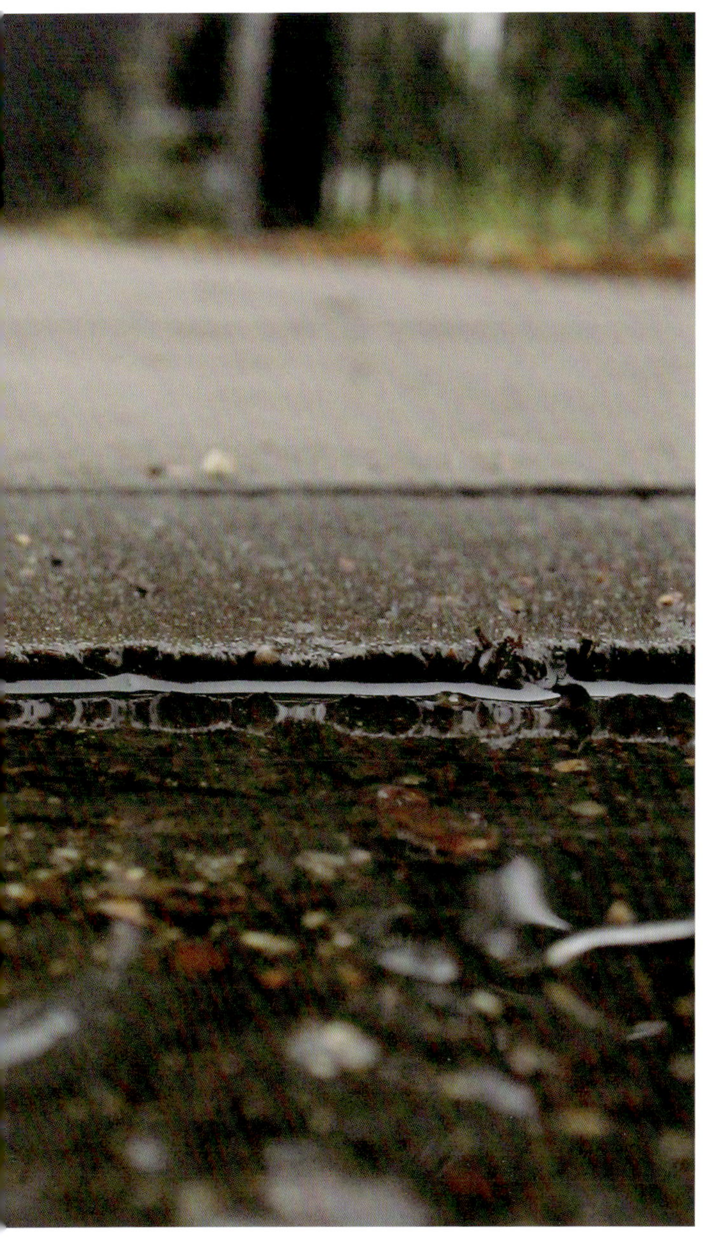

Skinny Dipping

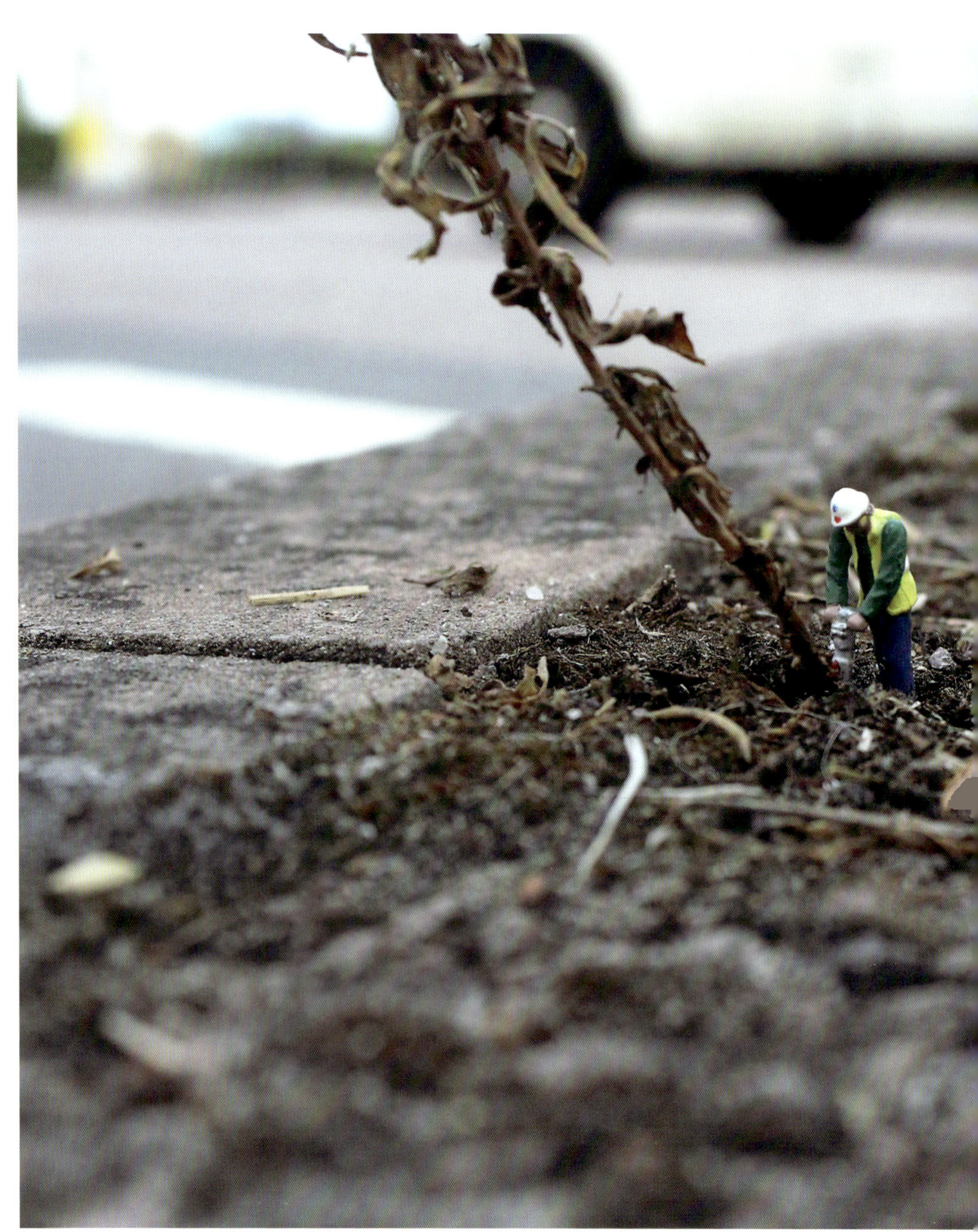

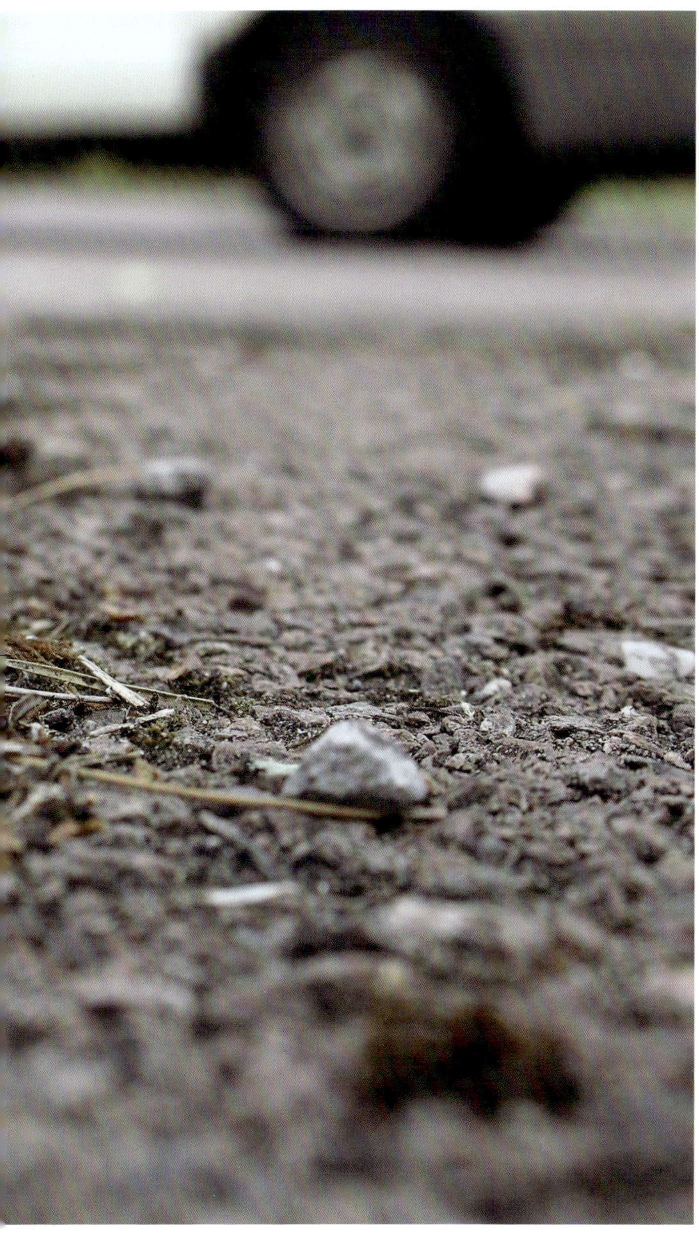

Deforestation

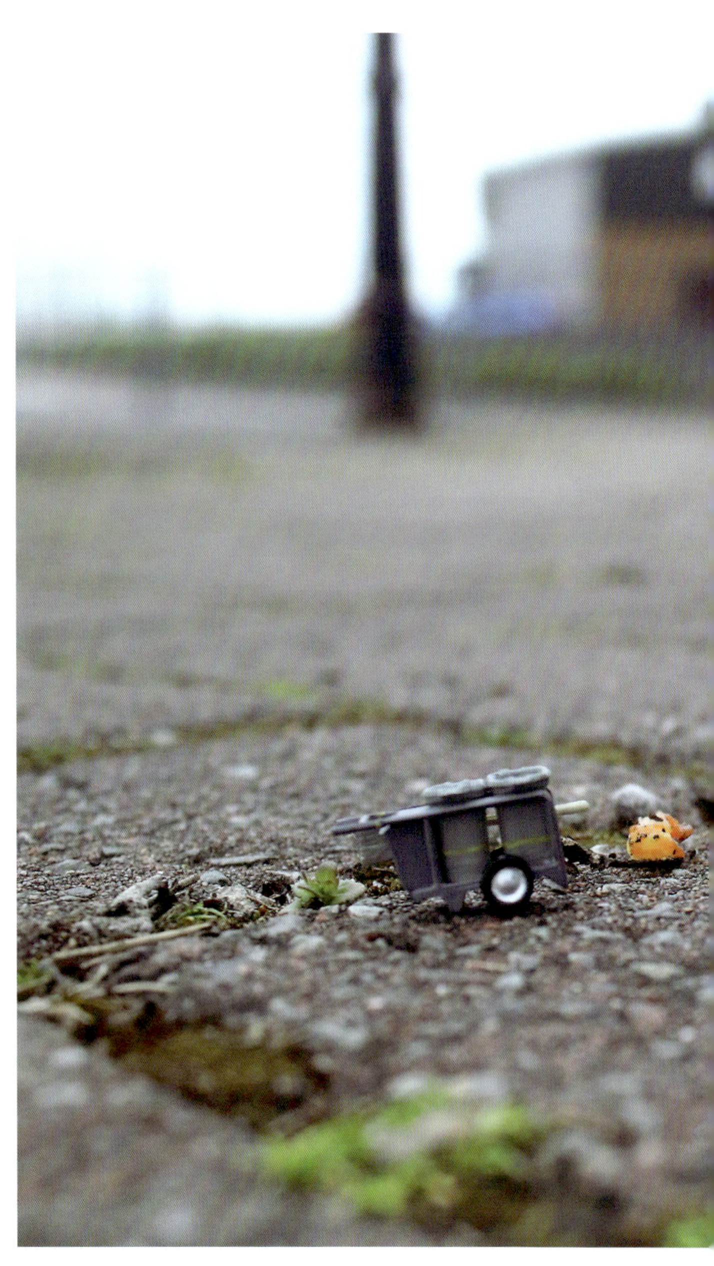

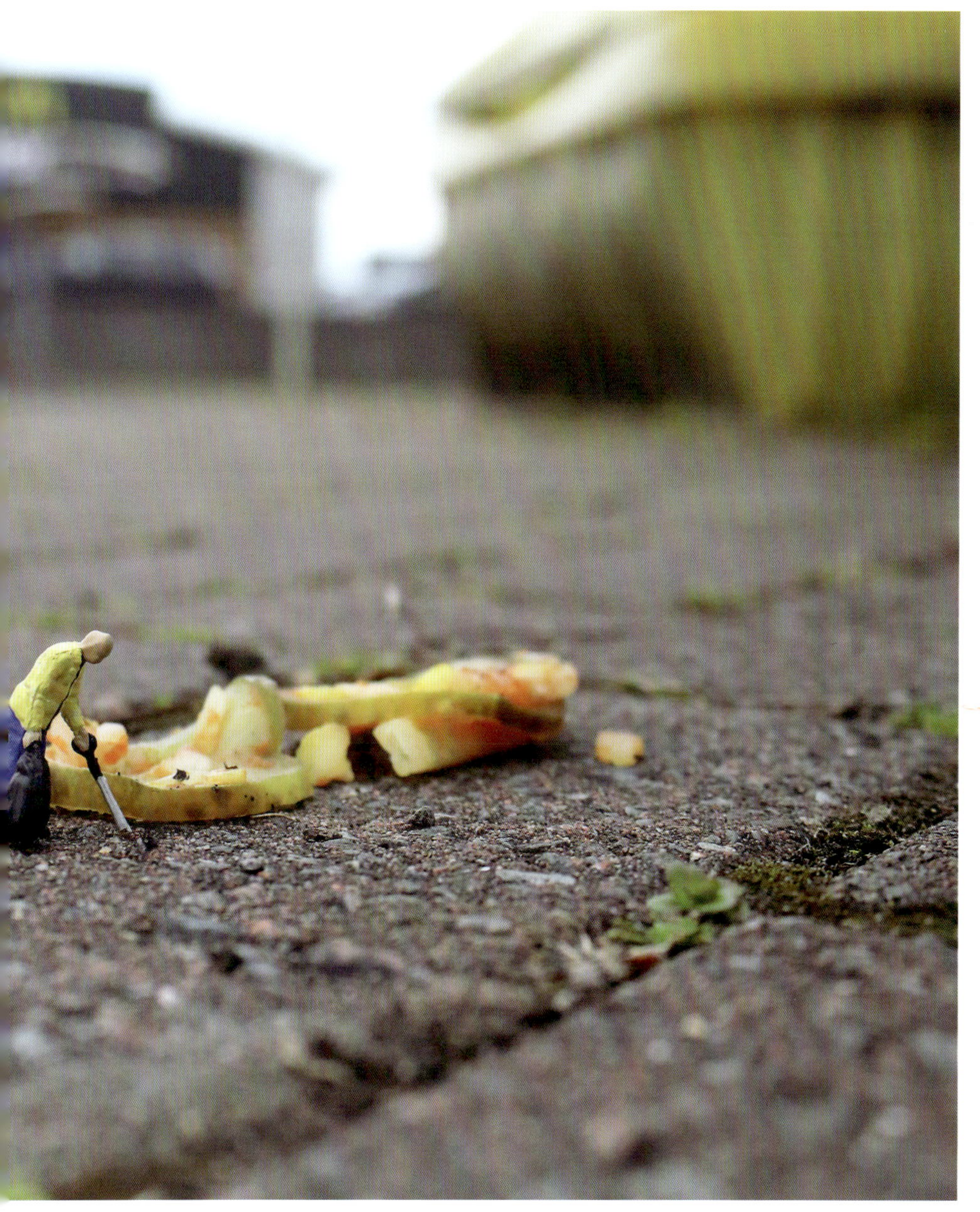

Gerkin Clean-Up

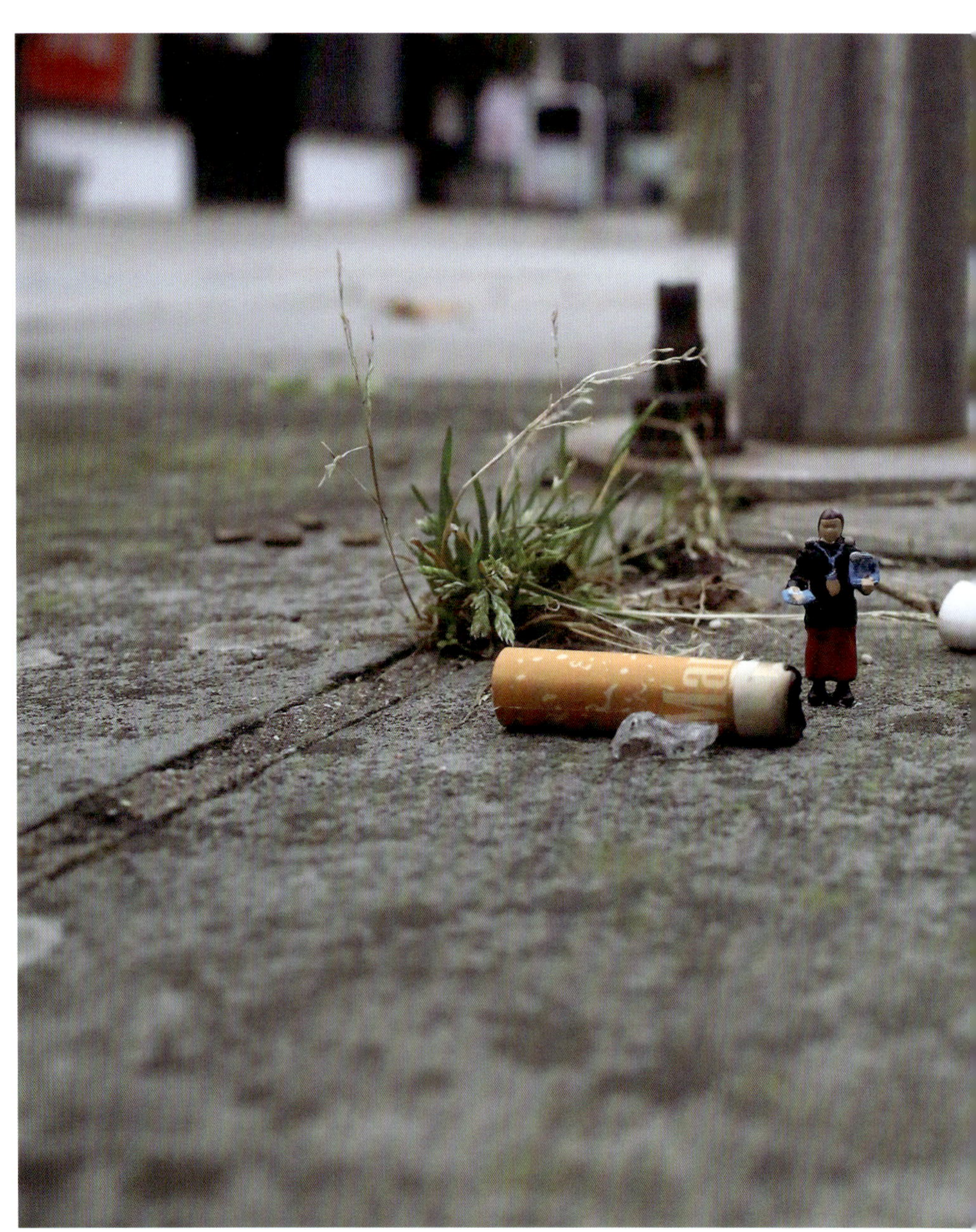

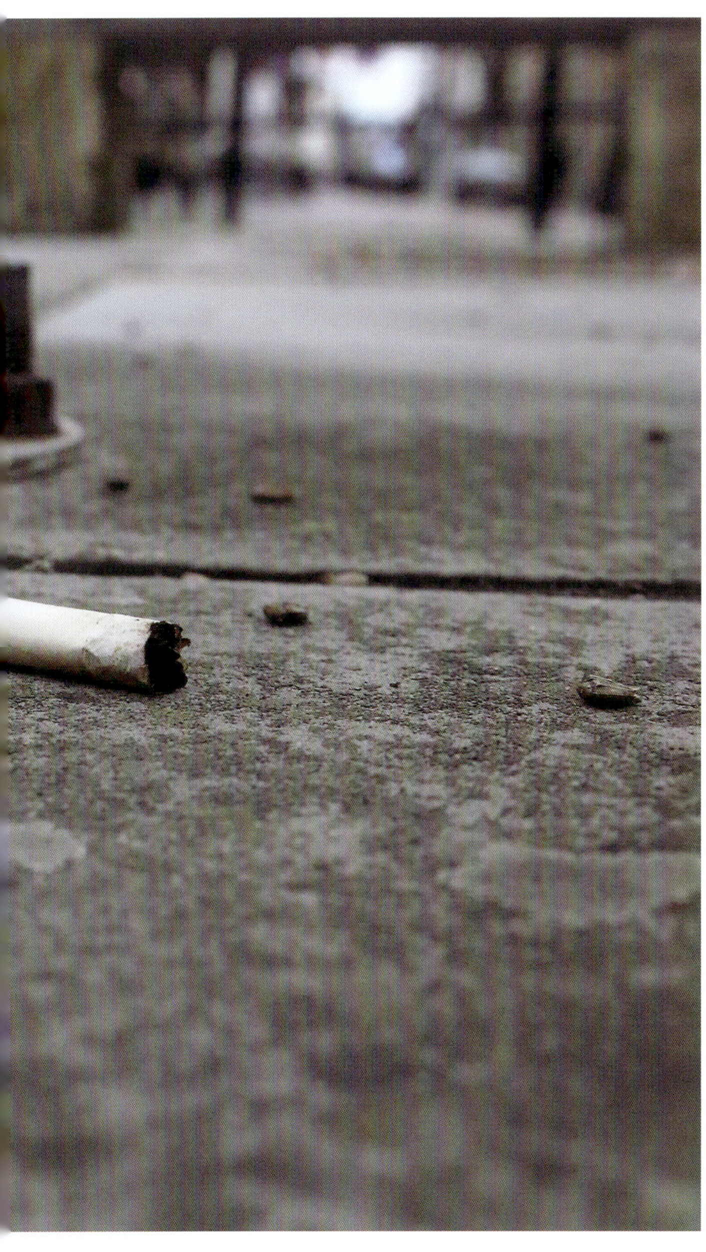

The Big Issue

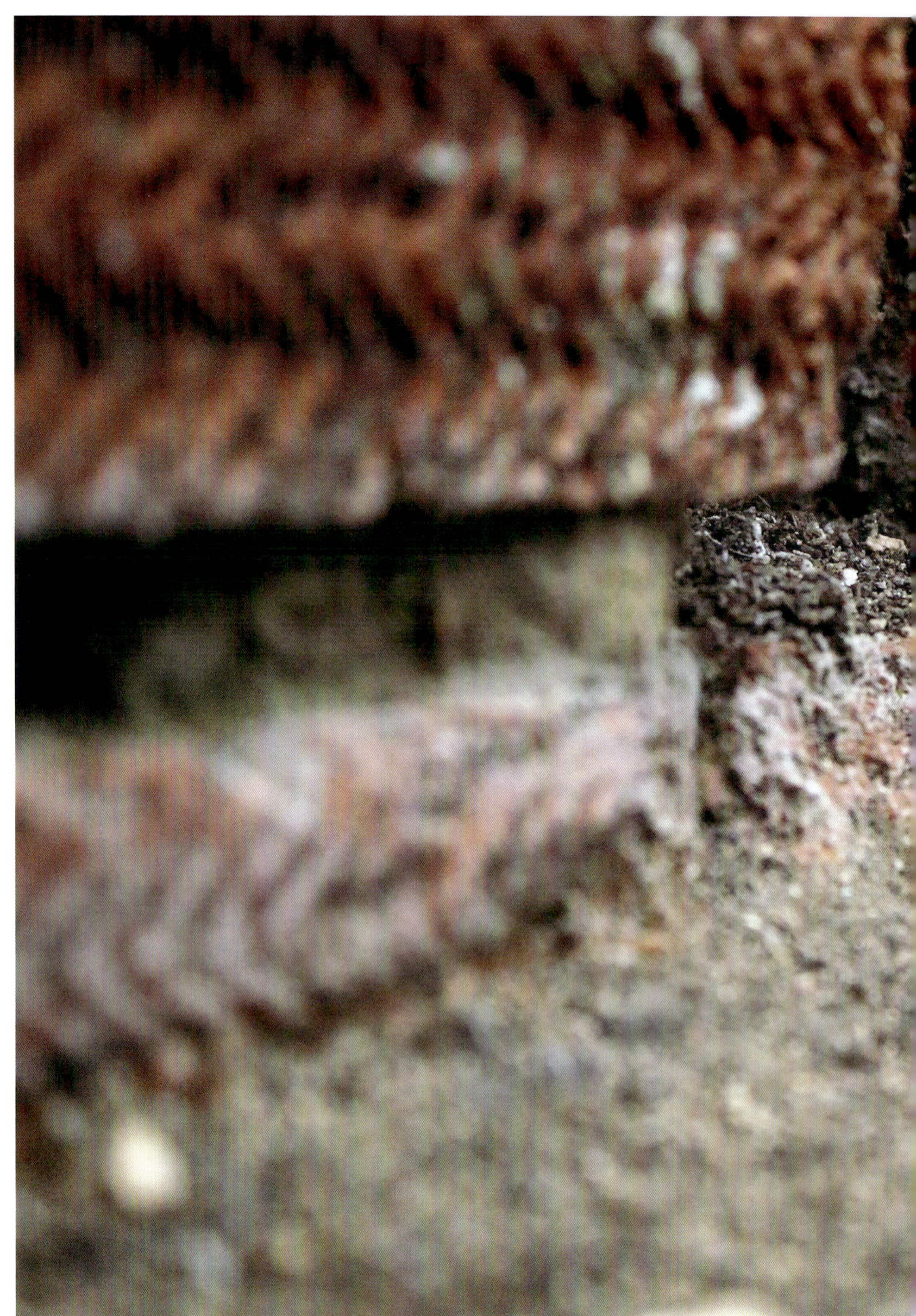

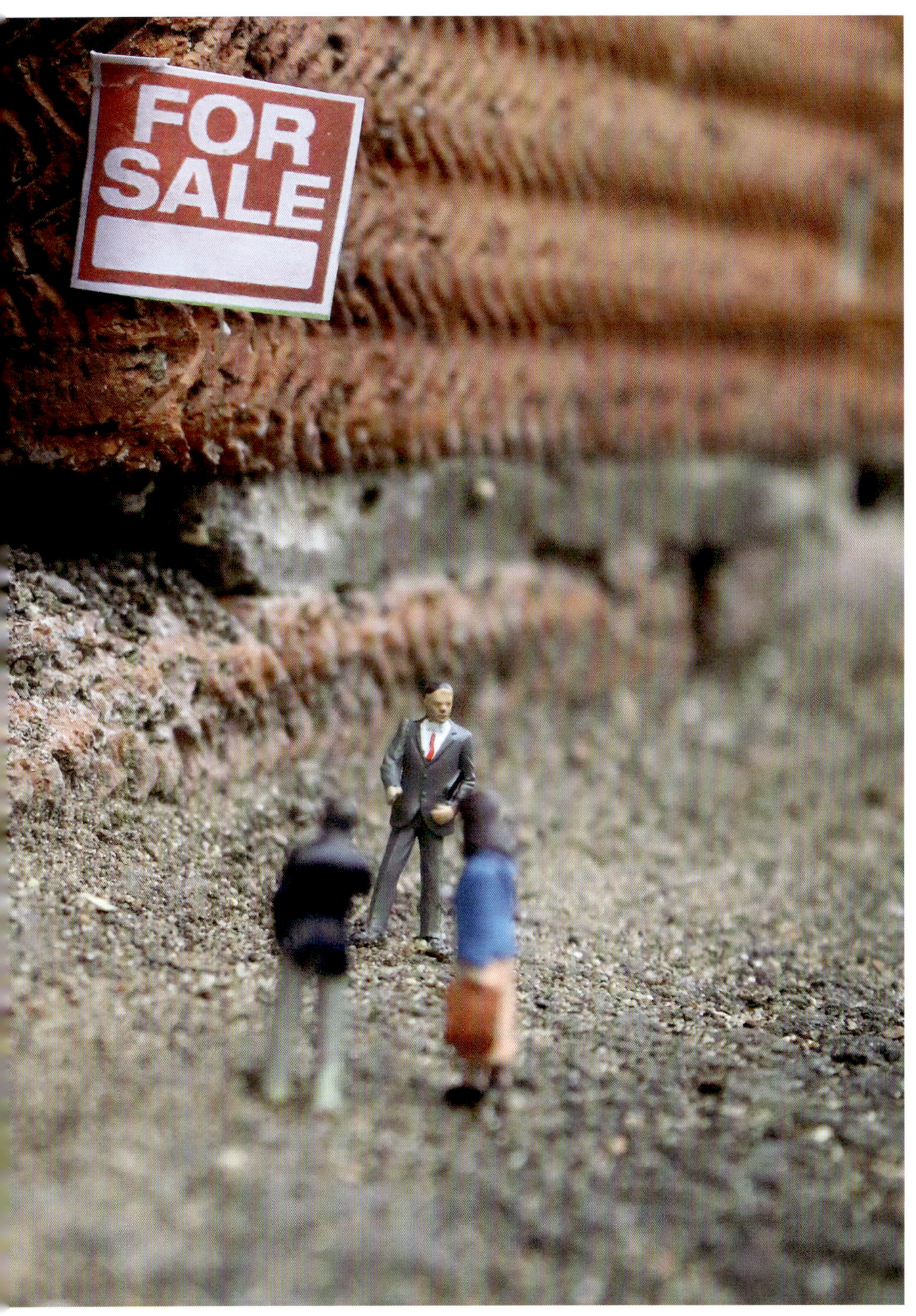

Location, Location, Location

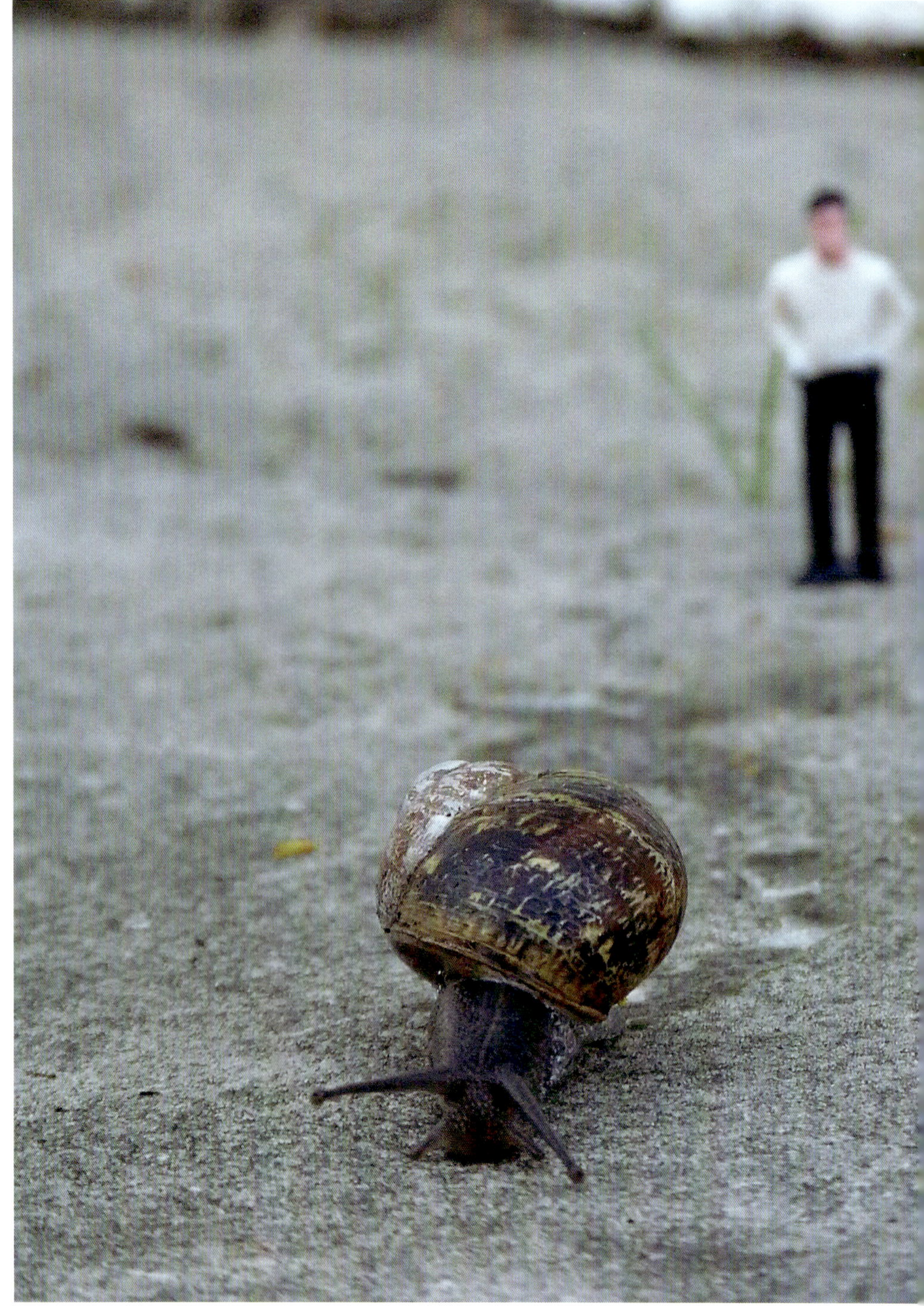

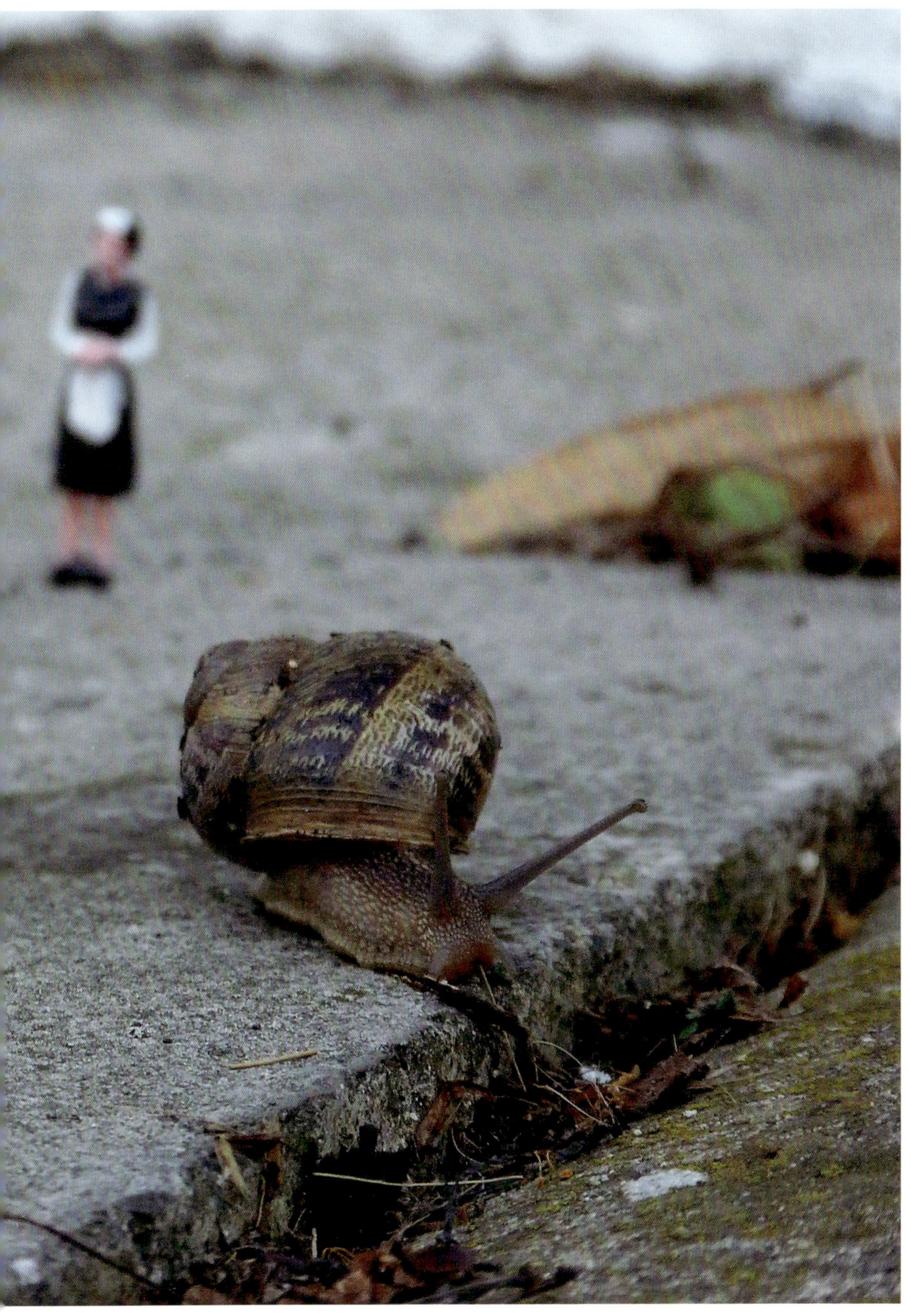

Invasion

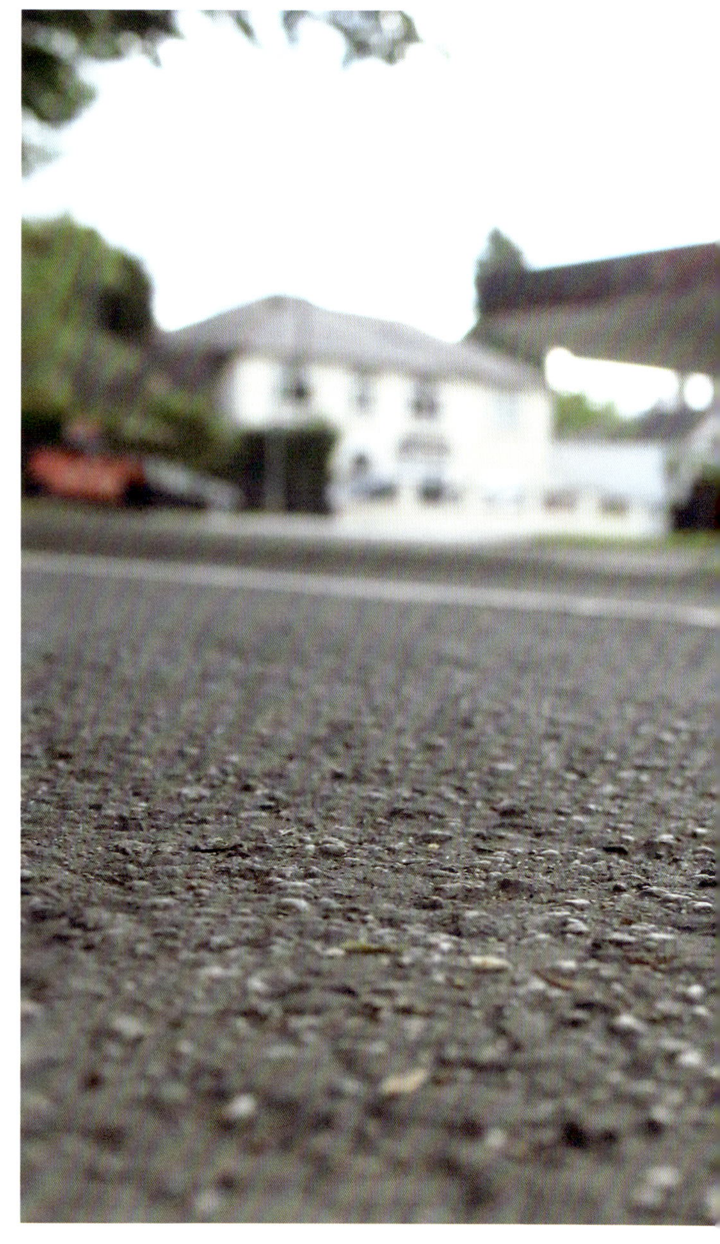

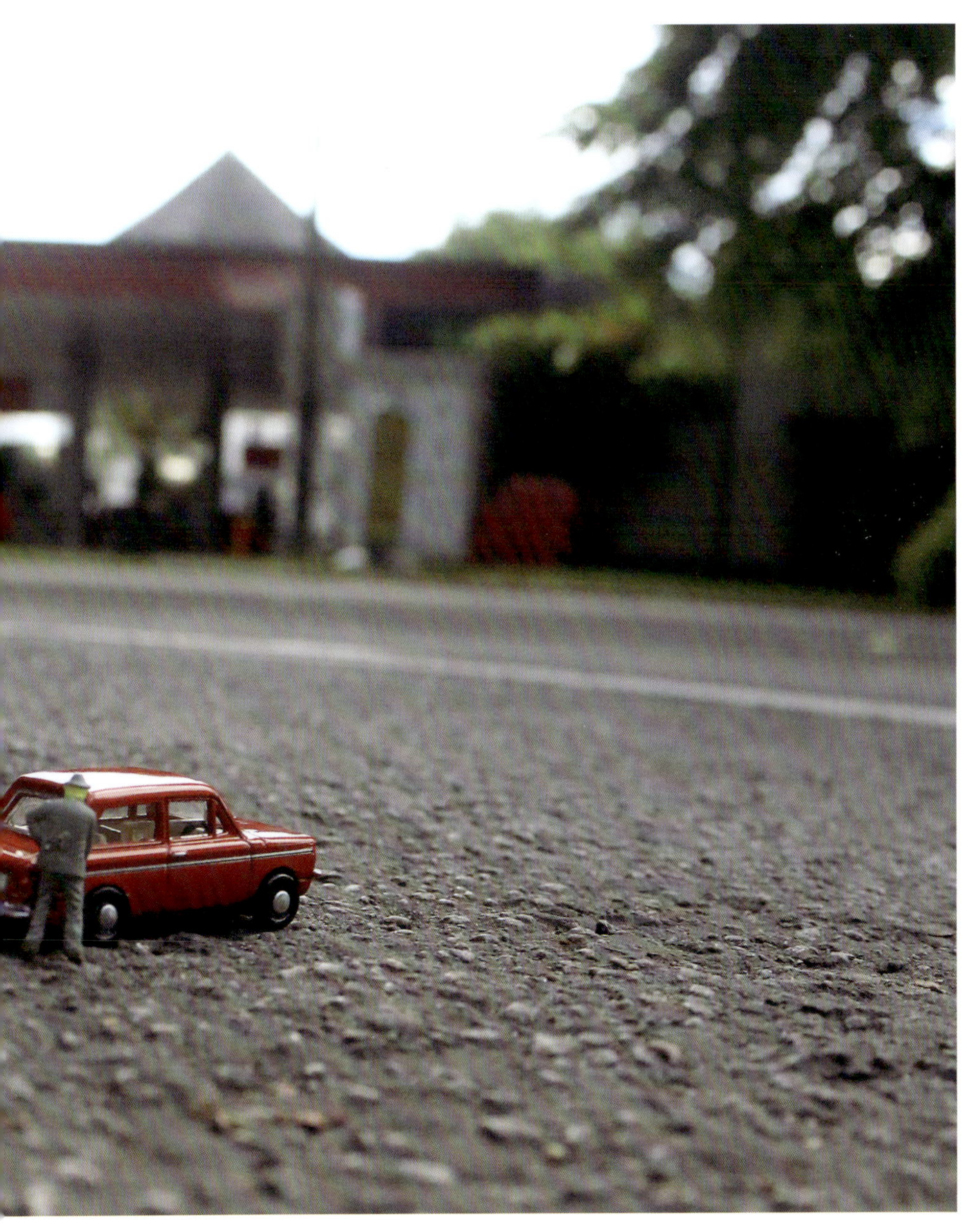

So Close, Yet So Far

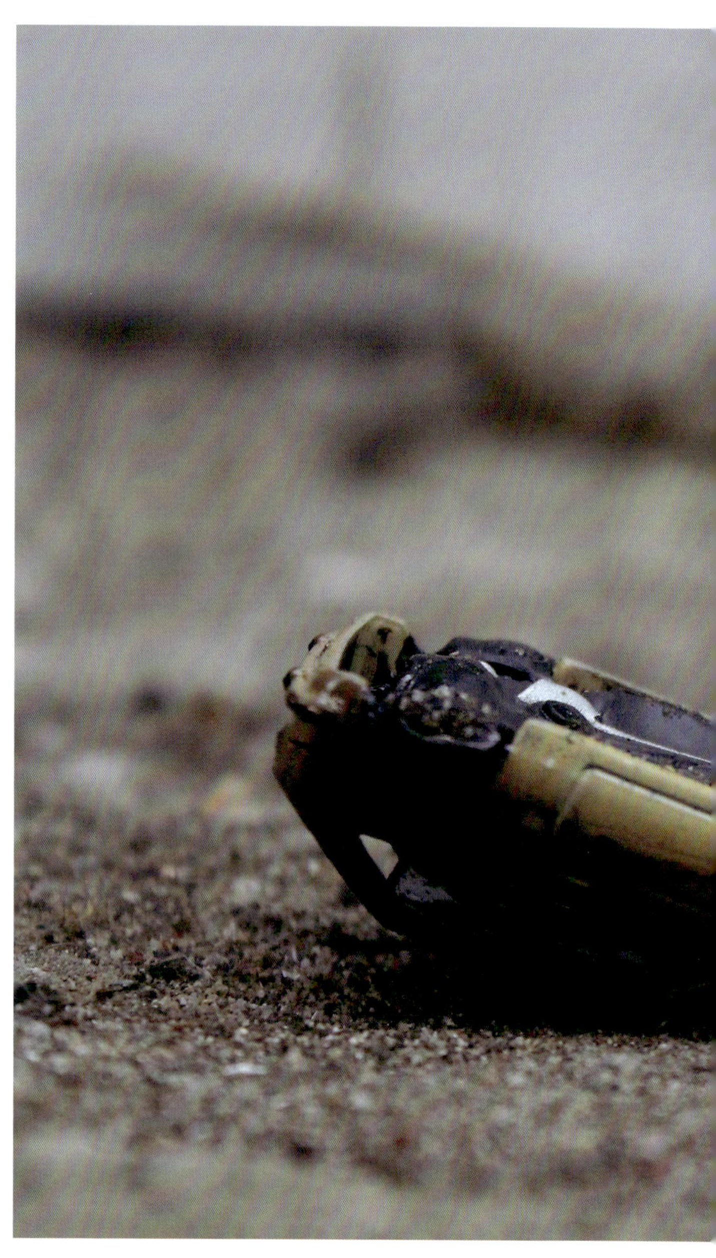

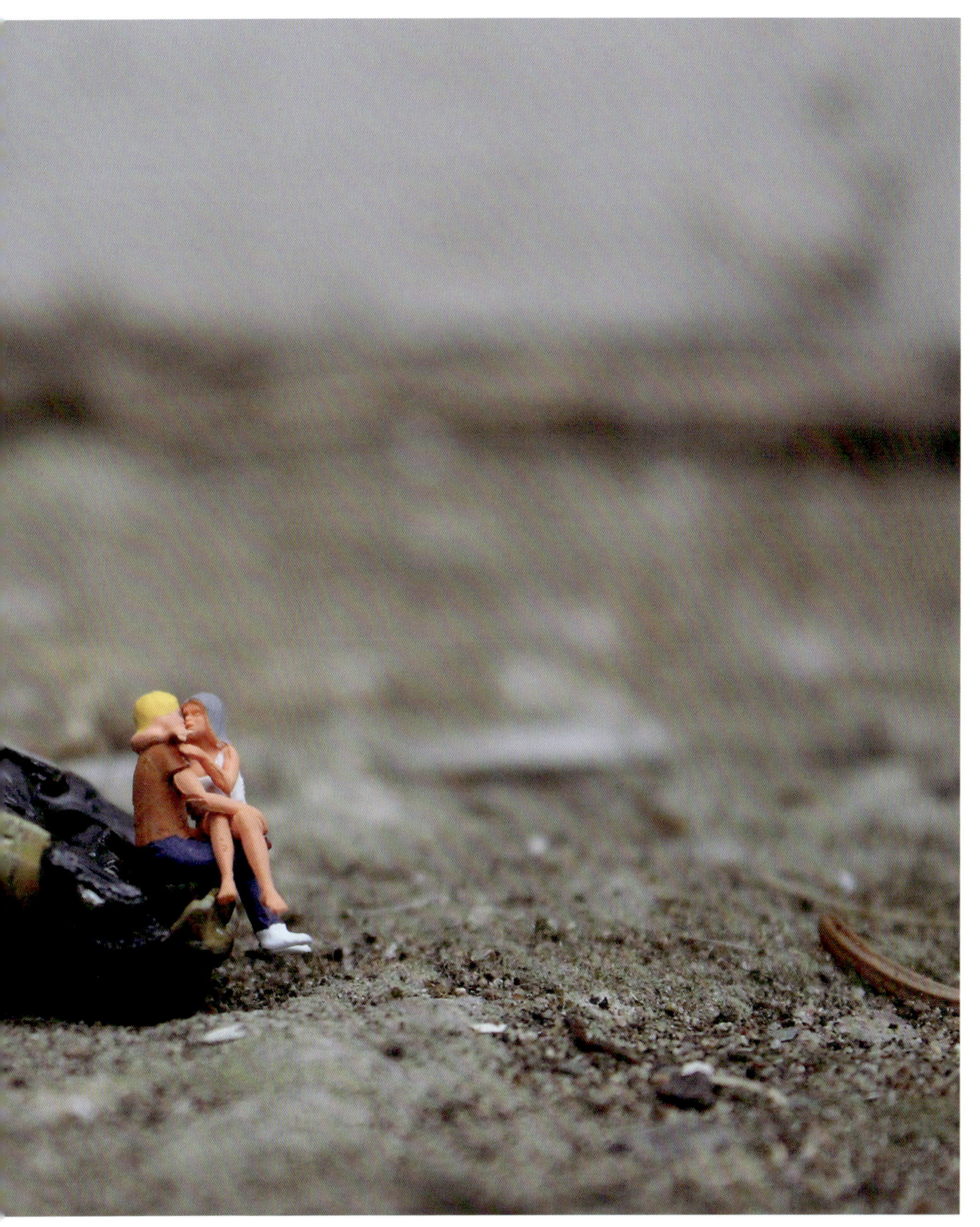

Love After Disaster

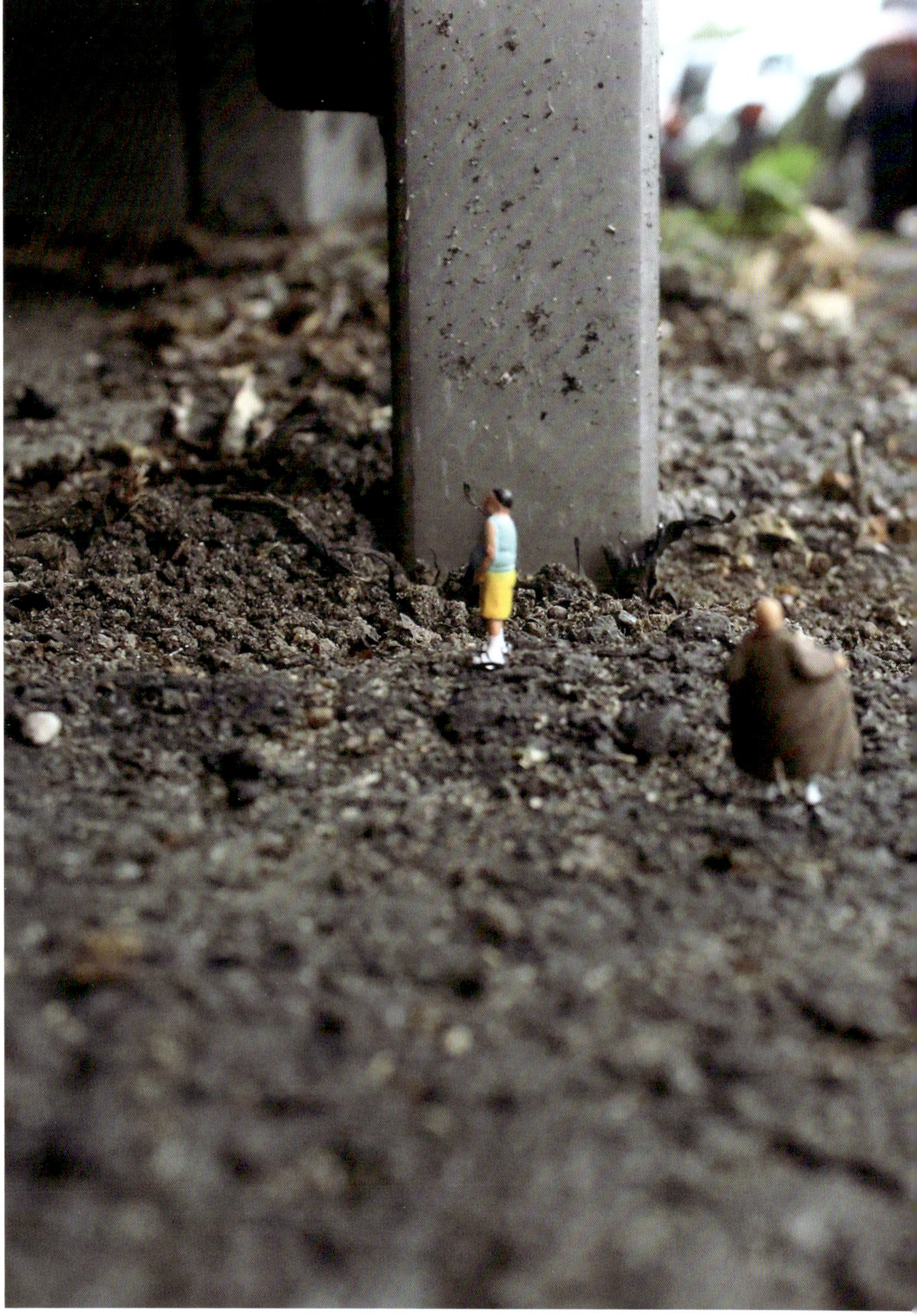

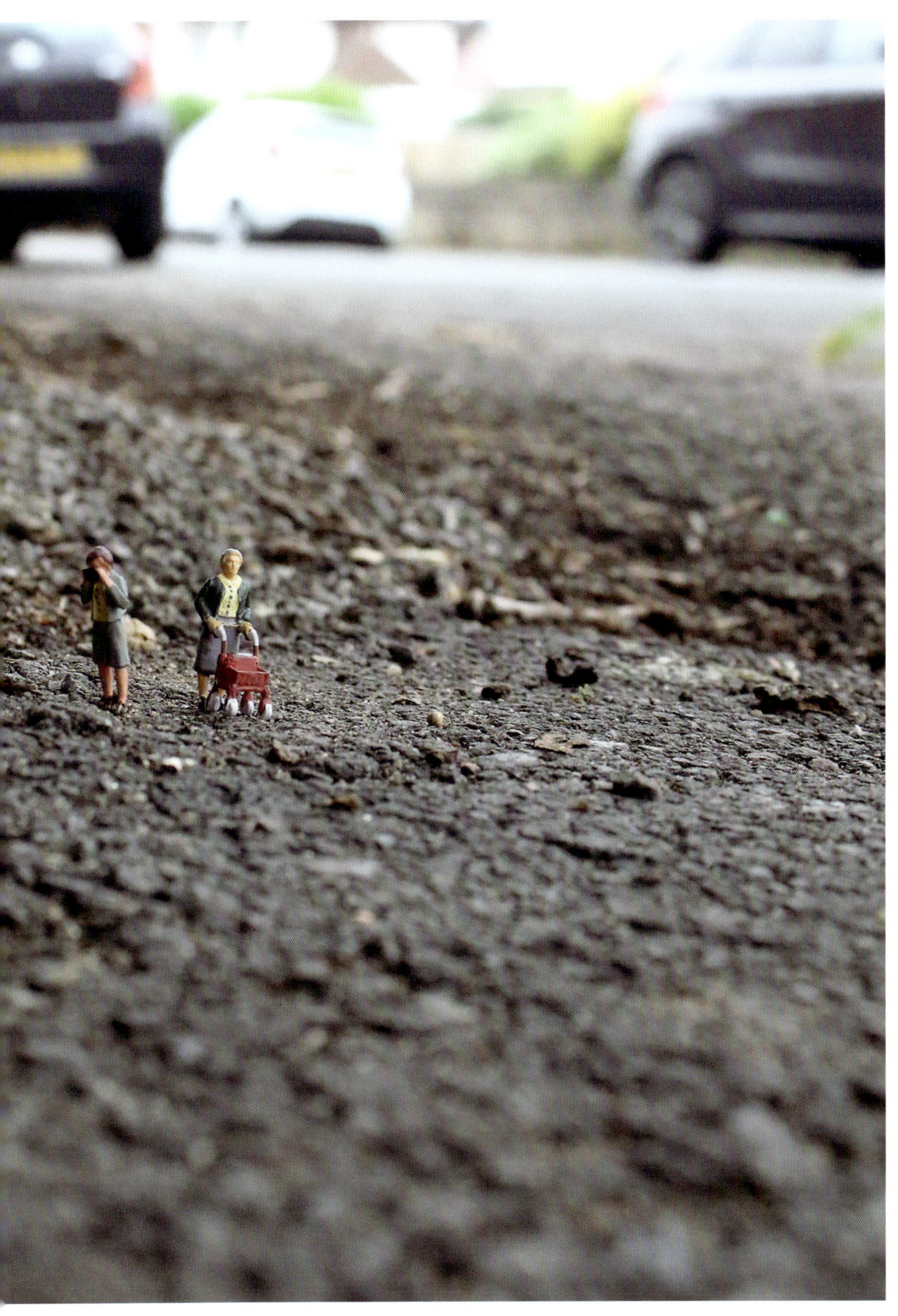

Another Day in the Neighborhood

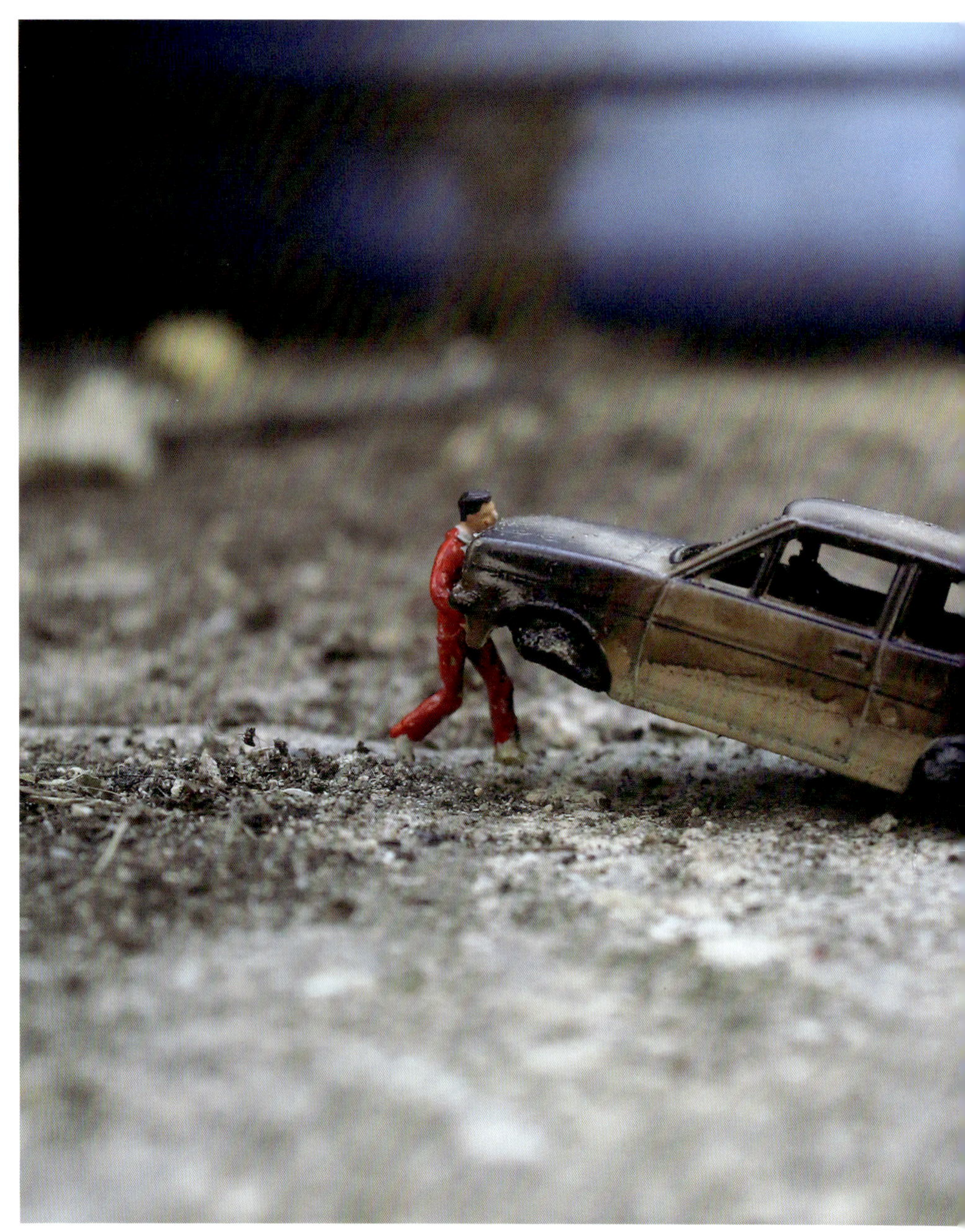

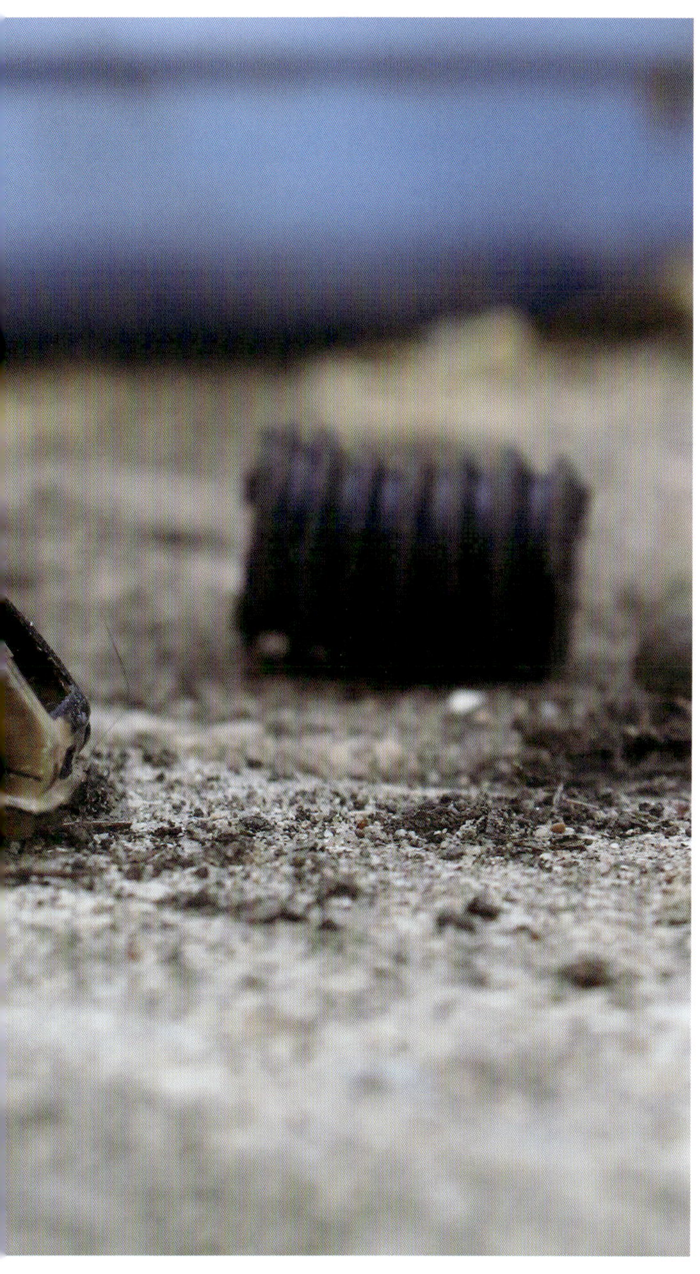

Olympic Training

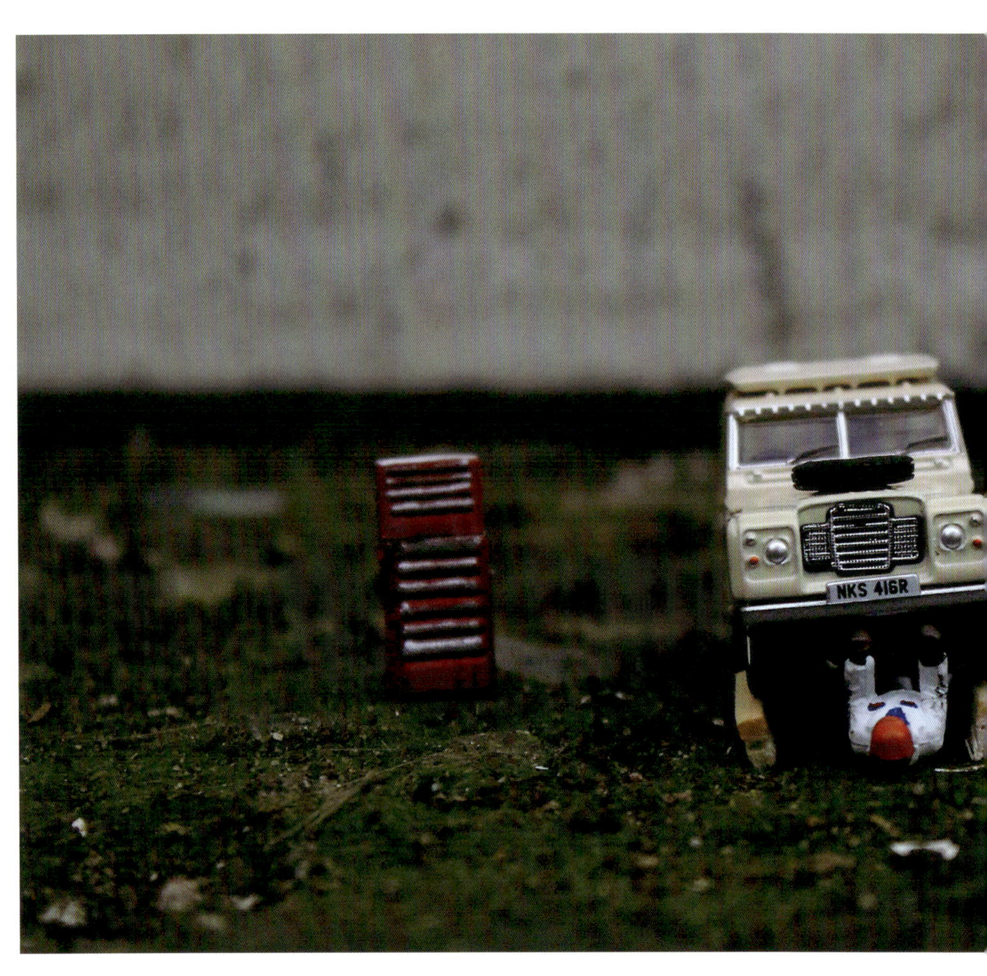
NKS 416R

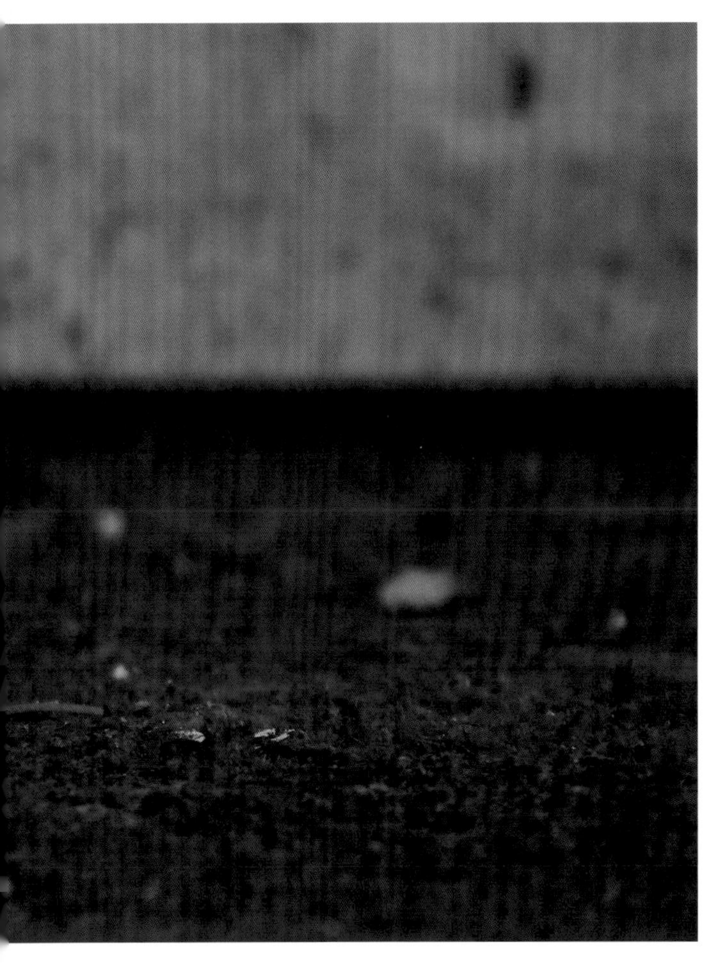

What Else Are Weekends For?

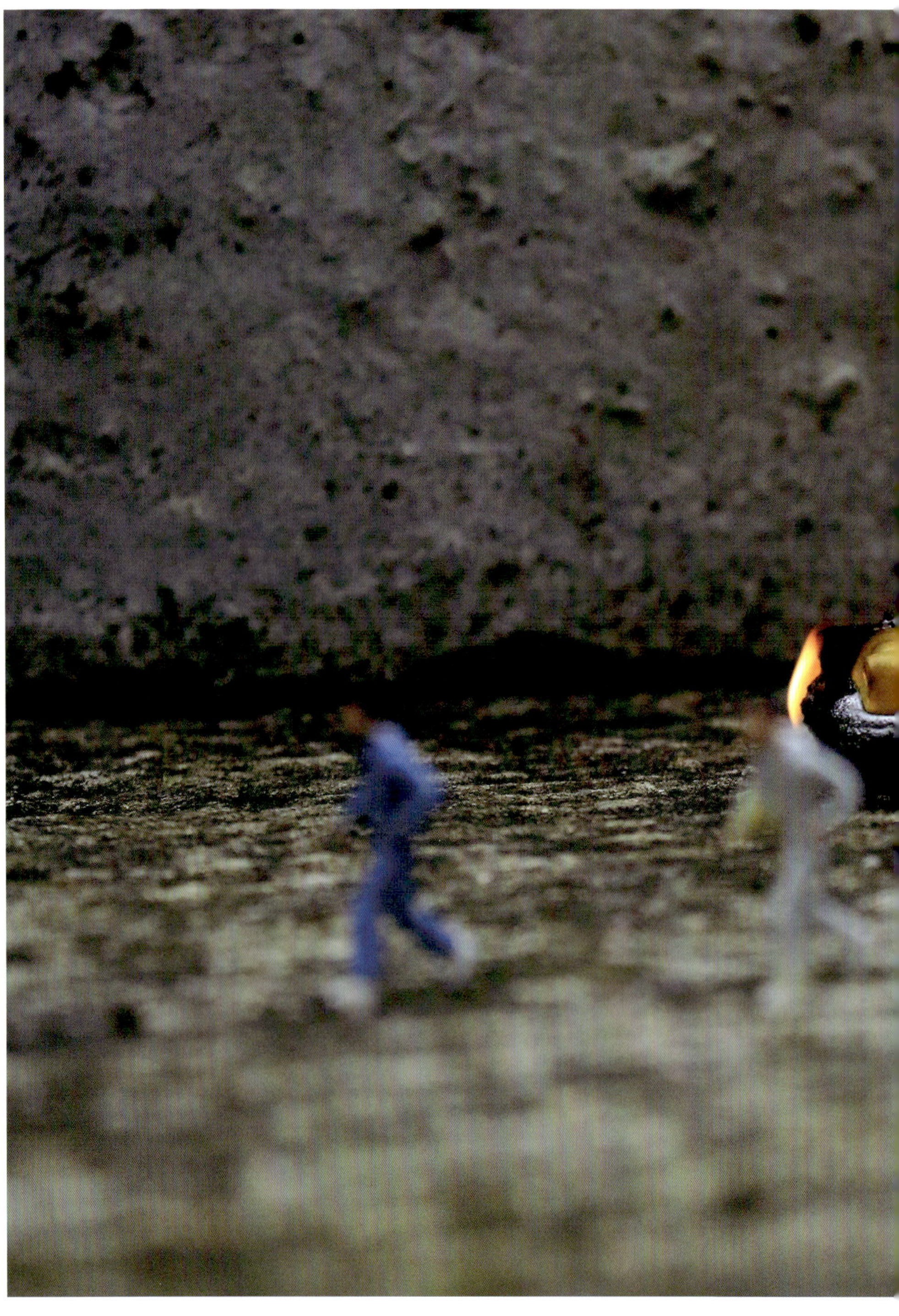

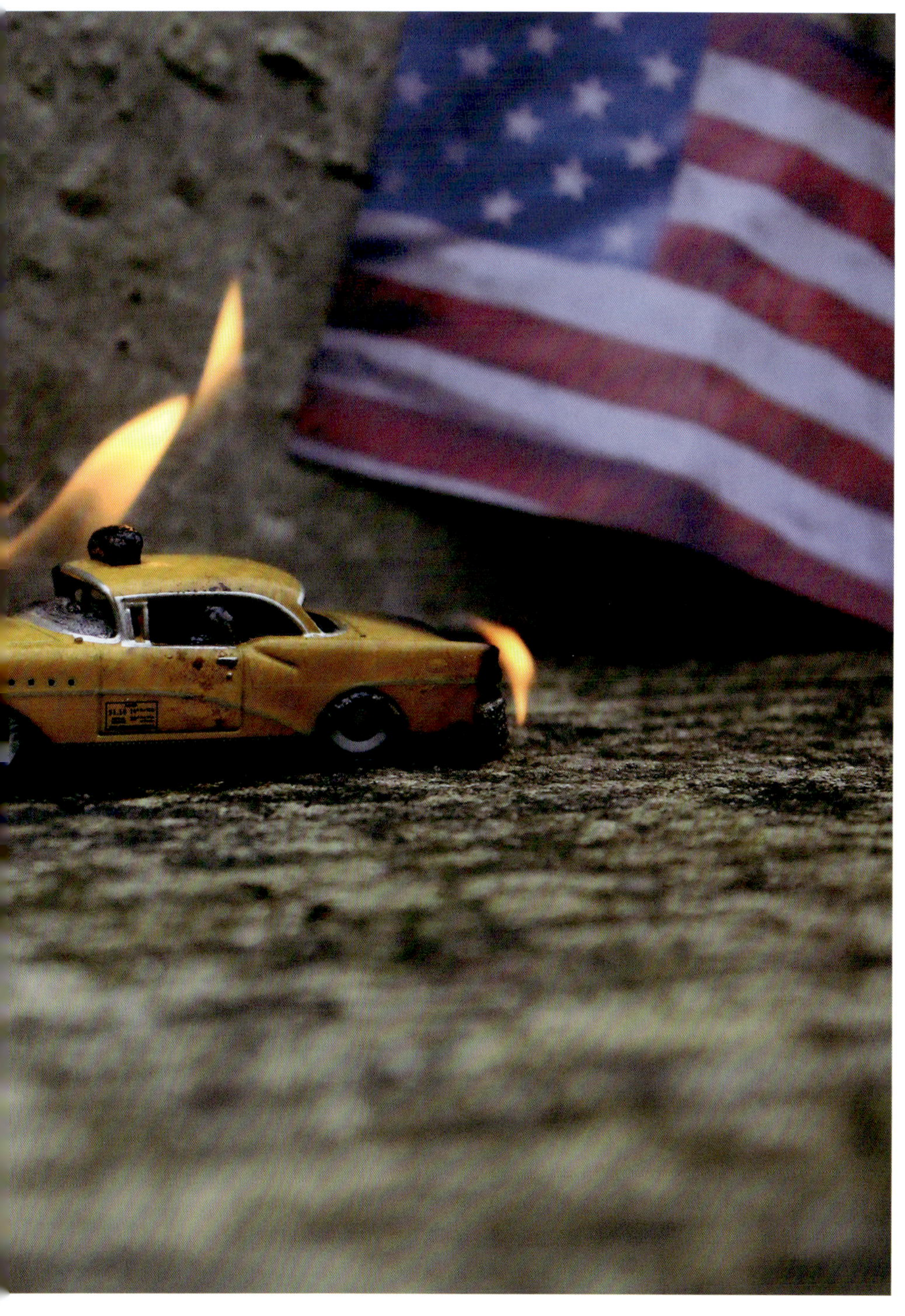

Riot

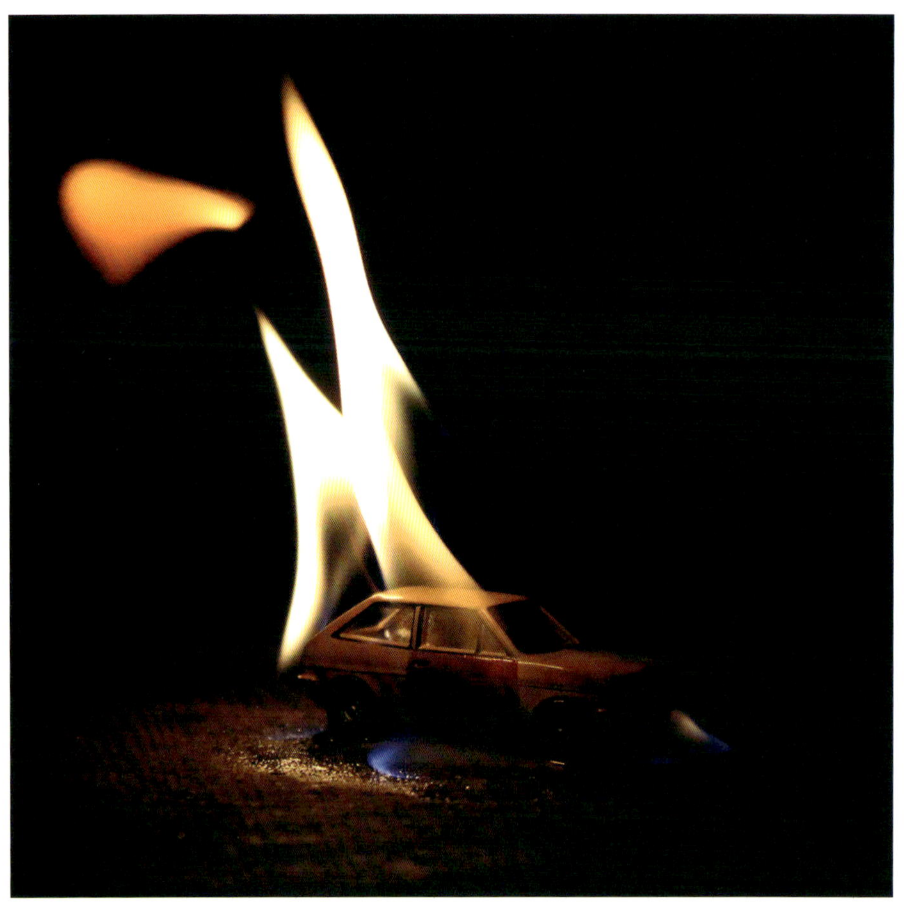

Destruction

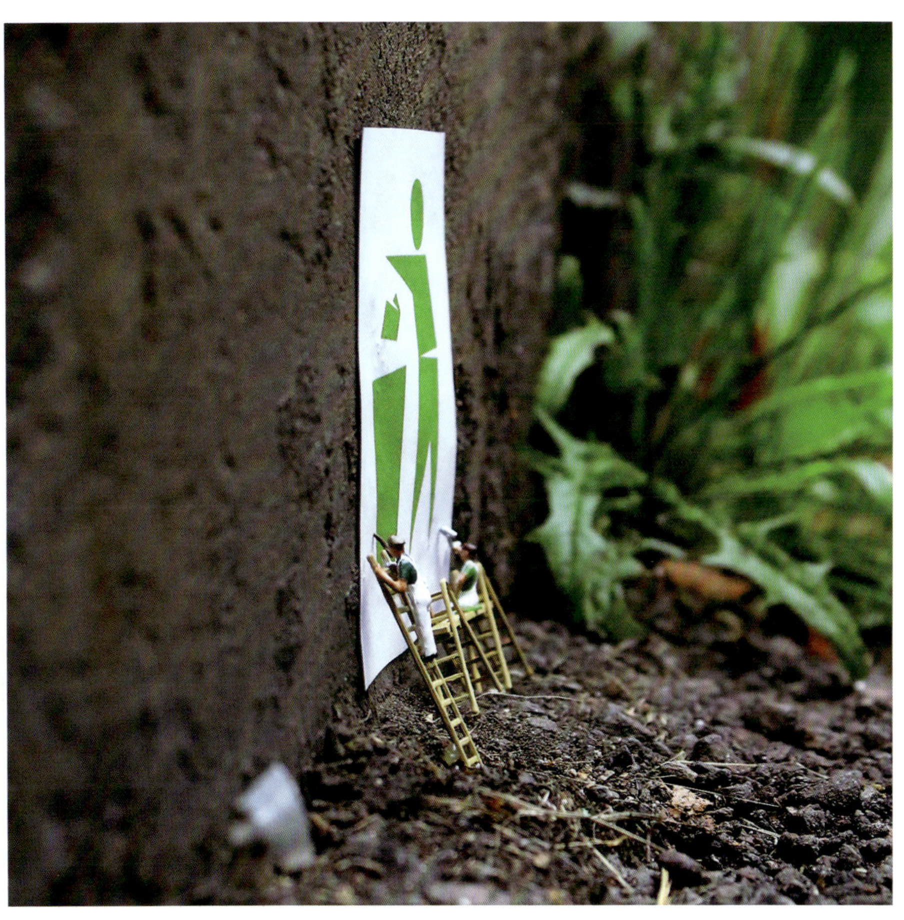

Keeping the Earth Tidy

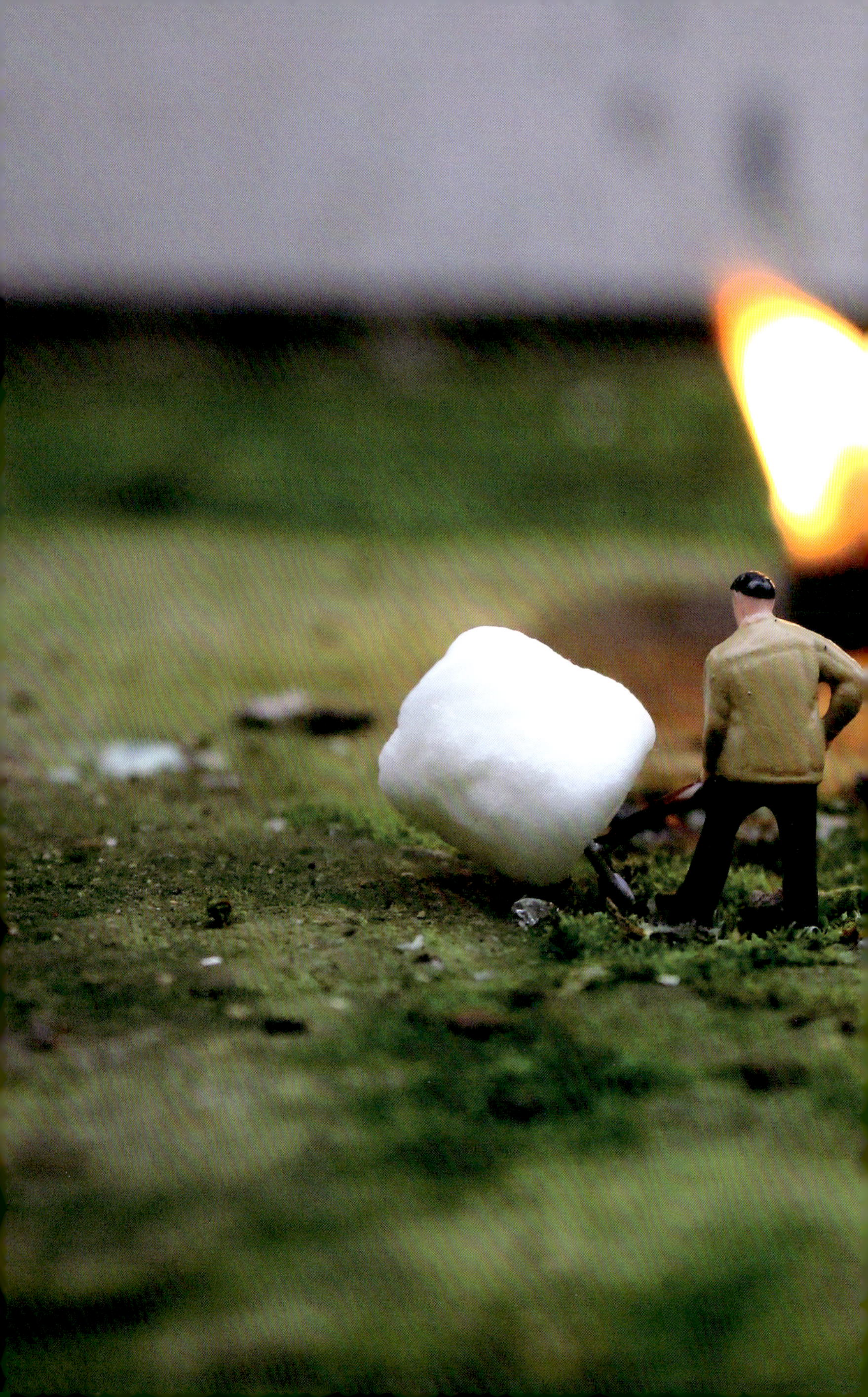

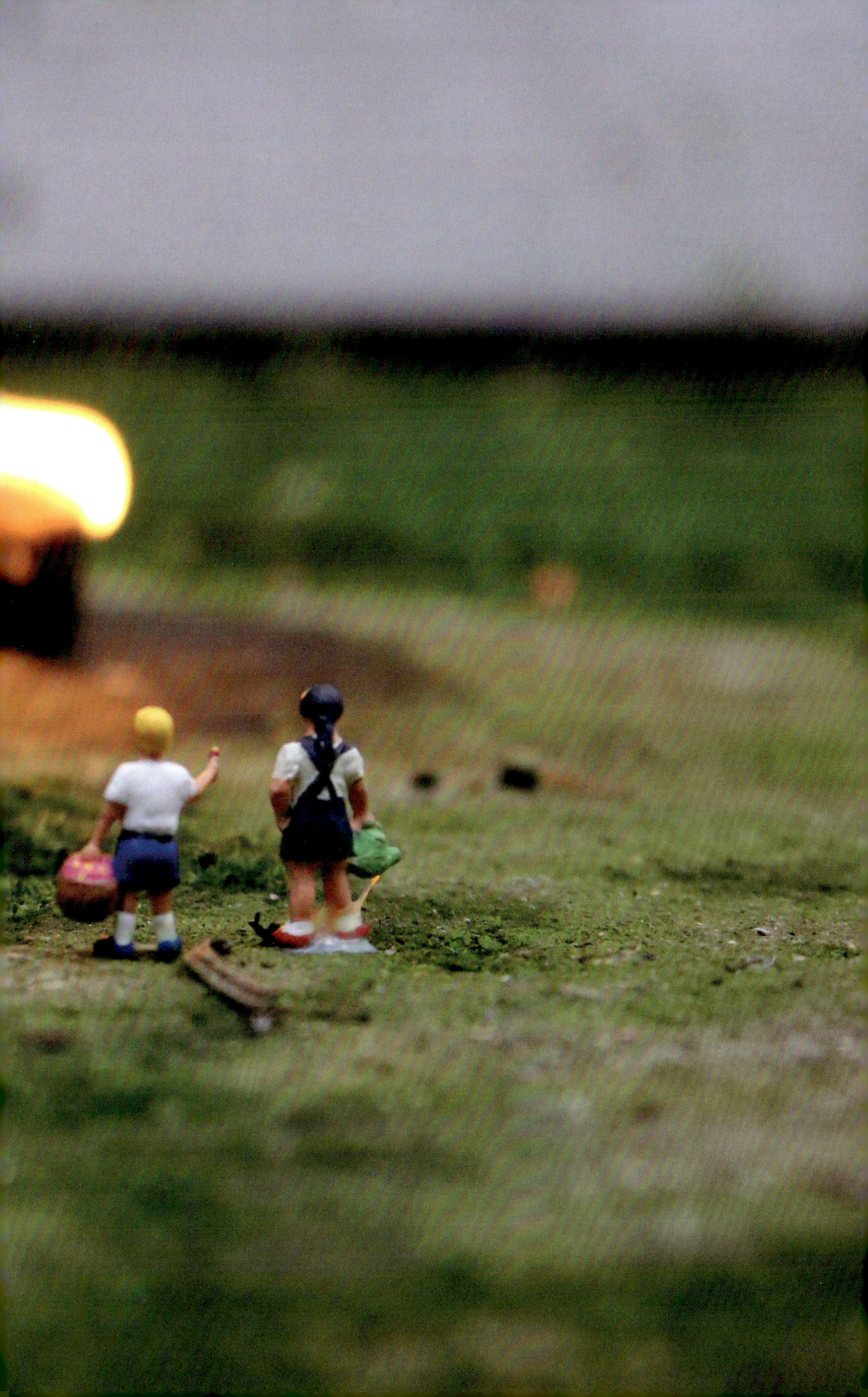

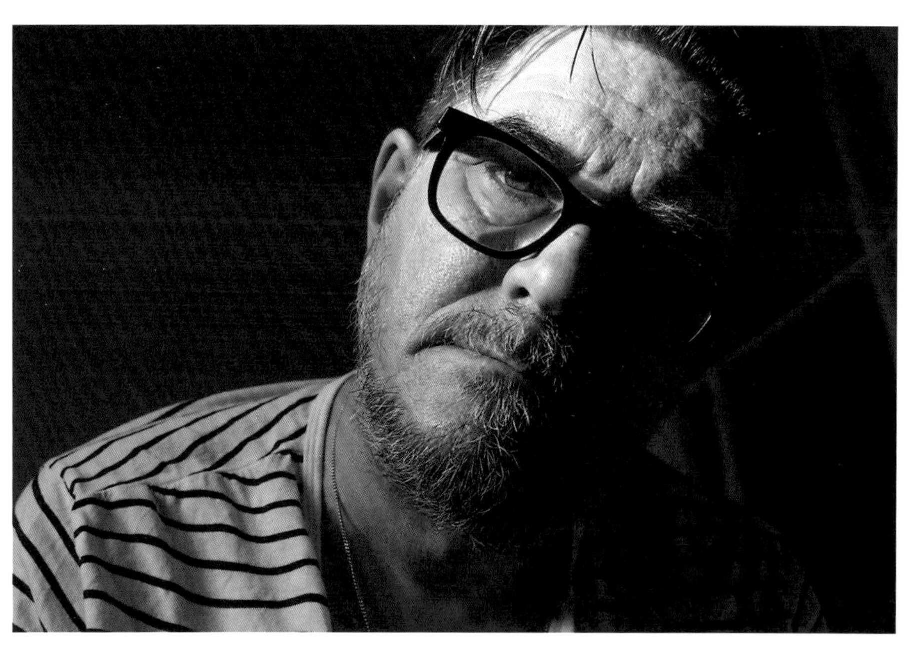

Steve Rolfe began his photography journey in 2010 while working as civil servant-office worker. Bored with the doldrums of his office job, his interest in photography was piqued when he saw a book of urban street photography images and was captivated by the scenes on each page. This led him to explore his own creativity through photography, borrowing his wife's Panasonic Lumix bridge camera to get started.

As a creative photographer, Steve always thinks outside the box and looks for inspiration in his own life. He is inspired by juxtaposition within his scene, always looking for something that appears out of place on a sidewalk or left in a gutter that shouldn't be there.

Now working as a full-time photographer, Steve's work has been published in multiple magazines, local and national newspapers. He lives and works in the beautiful countryside of Gloucestershire, England. *Small World* is his first book.

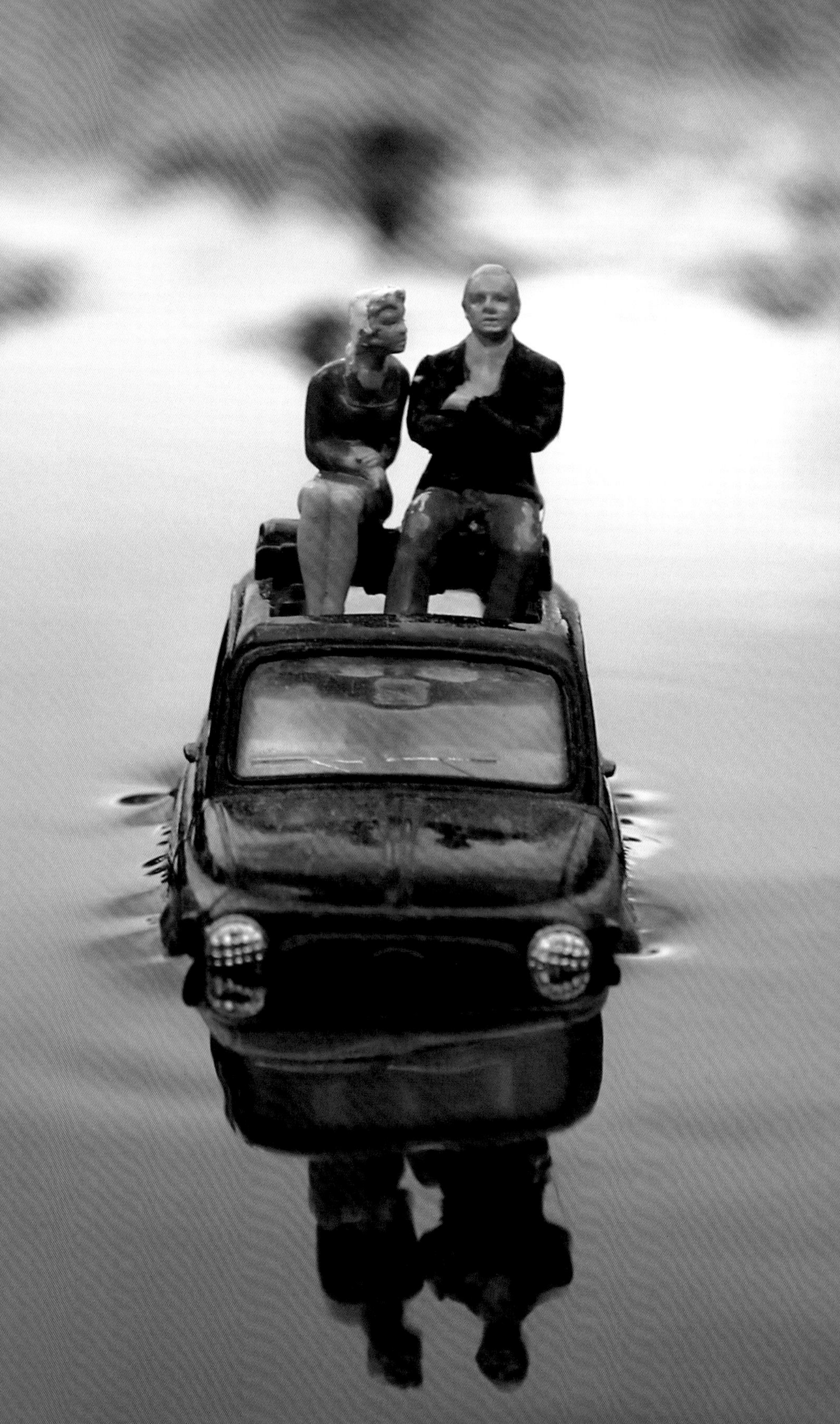

For my wife, Sallyann, for her constant support and for lending me the camera that got me started in photography.

Steve Rolfe

LCCN: 2022942178
ISBN: 978-1-9519631-0-1

Printed and bound in China
First printing, 2022

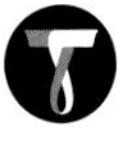

+ INFORMATION:
For additional information
on our books and prints,
visit trope.com

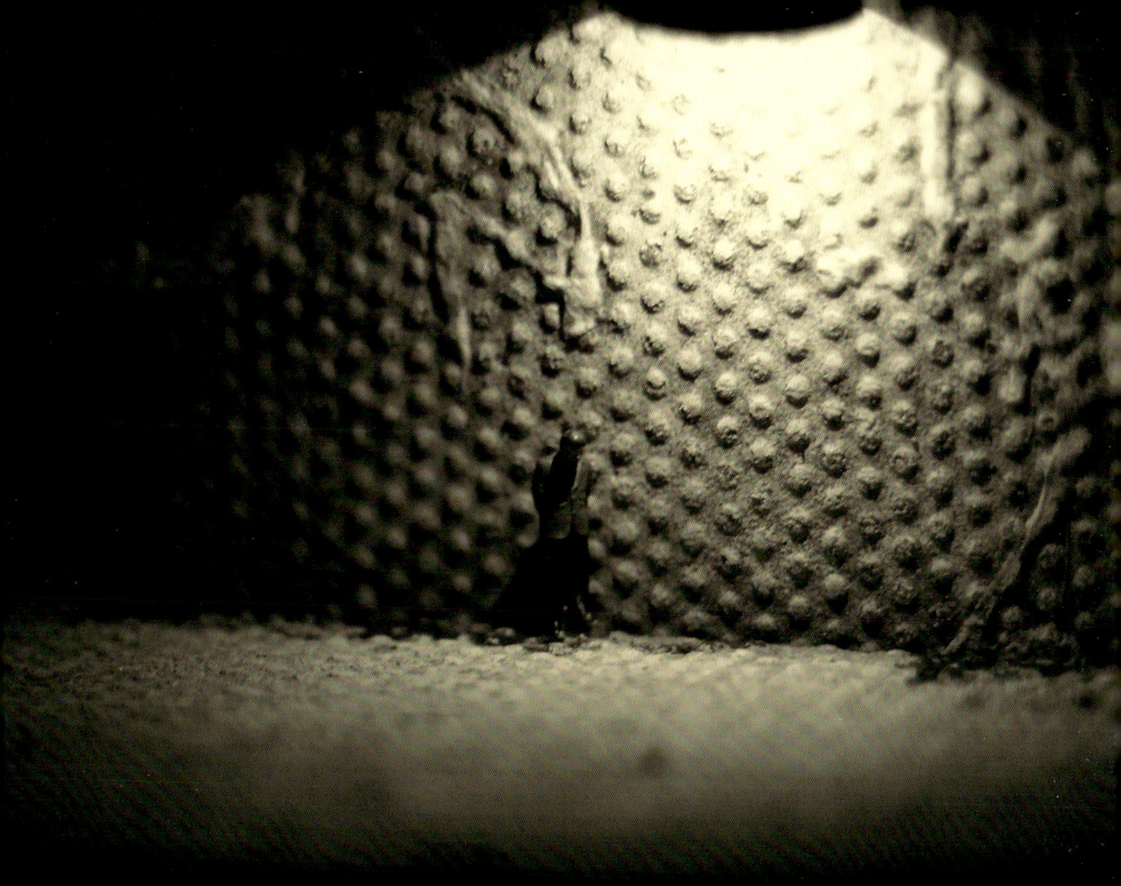

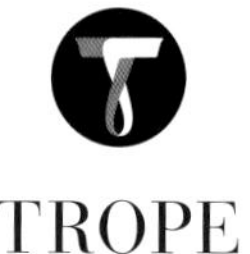

TROPE